MW00527857

How to Stay Safe Online

'Seyi Akiwowo's work to make the online world safer, especially for Black women, is not only powerful, it's necessary'
Nova Reid, anti-racism activist and author of *The Good Ally*

'Seyi Akiwowo is a force of nature and this book is a godsend. She exposes the depth and urgency of the online abuse crisis, explores the hypocrisy and inefficacy of tech companies and government, and explains what readers can do to improve their online lives. Accessible, empowering and potentially life-changing, this is a book everyone should read'
Laura Bates, author of *Men Who Hate Women* and *Girl Up*, and founder of the Everyday Sexism Project

'I wish the Internet was a safer place, but until that day comes, this helpful book is a crucial companion. How wonderful to have Seyi on our side as we navigate through the stormy seas of the online world which she, sadly, knows all too well. The brilliant tools in this book will help you set better boundaries, protect your mental health, be a better digital citizen, and in general look after ourselves and each other'
Emma Gannon, *Sunday Times* bestselling author of *The Multi-Hyphen Method*

ABOUT THE AUTHOR

Seyi Akiwowo is the founder of Glitch, a UK charity making digital spaces safe for all by ending online abuse. Before setting up Glitch, Seyi was elected as the youngest Black female councillor in east London at the age of twenty-three.

A graduate of the London School of Economics, Seyi spoke on 'Fixing the Glitch' at TedxLondon in 2019 and appeared on *Wired's* front cover as their top Changemaker of 2021.

How to Stay Safe Online

A Digital Self-Care Toolkit for
Developing Resilience and Allyship

SEYI AKIWOWO

PENGUIN LIFE

AN IMPRINT OF

PENGUIN BOOKS

PENGUIN LIFE

UK | USA | Canada | Ireland | Australia
India | New Zealand | South Africa

Penguin Life is part of the Penguin Random House group of companies
whose addresses can be found at global.penguinrandomhouse.com.

Penguin
Random House
UK

First published 2022
001

Copyright © Seyi Akiwowo, 2022

The moral right of the author has been asserted

Text design by Alice Woodward
Set in 10.25/14pt Gill Sans MT Pro
Typeset by Jouve (UK), Milton Keynes
Printed and bound in Great Britain by Clays Ltd, Elcograf S.p.A.

The authorized representative in the EEA is Penguin Random House Ireland,
Morrison Chambers, 32 Nassau Street, Dublin D02 YH68

A CIP catalogue record for this book is available from the British Library

ISBN: 978-0-241-53521-9

www.greenpenguin.co.uk

MIX
Paper from
responsible sources
FSC® C018179

Penguin Random House is committed to a
sustainable future for our business, our readers
and our planet. This book is made from Forest
Stewardship Council® certified paper.

To Oluwaseyi Akiwowo, the seven-year-old girl who had to grow up fast to survive a cruel world, and to twenty-six-year-old Seyi, who weathered a dark and scary storm of online abuse.

We are now thriving!
x

Contents

Contents

Contents

Contents

Introduction

Picture this: it's an early morning in February. A young Black woman is on a treadmill, pleased with herself for still being committed to her New Year's resolution. After she takes an obligatory #gymselfie at the very same leisure centre where she learned to swim and took part in secondary-school PE, she puts in the earphones connected to her phone and presses play on her gym playlist. The next song up is a club banger, 'Work' by Rihanna (featuring Drake). But, strangely, the song keeps dipping in and out. Confused and distracted, the young woman pauses the treadmill. She picks up her phone to investigate, ready to complain that her Spotify Premium subscription isn't providing a premium service at all. She freezes. A crushing wave of panic and then denial crashes over her as she watches a waterfall of notifications cascade down the screen. She manages to catch some of the previews:

'Ni**a.'
'A talking ape?'
'Which STD will end your miserable life?'
'Ni**eress.'
'I hope you get lynched you nog.'
'Slit your clitoris.'
'hahahahahaha eat shit'

The leisure centre – until moments ago a place full of joyful childhood memories – feels immediately unsafe. She looks around, panicking, unsure of who to speak to, who can help, unclear of what to do next, all while frantically wondering what she has even done wrong.

That young Black woman is me.

I wish I could say this is the plot of a Netflix drama I've made up to help you better understand the impact of online abuse. But it isn't. It's a snippet of my story. I was elected as East London's youngest Black female councillor in 2014, and this – my first unprepared reckoning with online patriarchy and white supremacy – happened three years later. A video of my speech at the European Parliament had gone viral, and with that attention I became the subject of people's unfiltered hatred. I experienced very real, very serious threats to my safety and well-being. The cold and lonely sense of powerlessness was overwhelming. After that painful experience, I ambitiously (and naively) began campaigning to hold tech giants accountable for the millions of women facing or fearing online abuse.

Like most people thrown into the dark side of the internet, I was largely ill-equipped to handle it. My loved ones didn't know what to do or how best to support me. They made well-meaning suggestions to delete my account or make it private, rather than focusing on what was – and still is – a massive, systemic and global problem: online abuse. One that's going ignored or is actively swept under the rug by social media platforms. One that is nowhere near the top of the political agenda, despite the significant impact online abuse has on democracy, social cohesion, security, human rights and people's well-being.

I became a survivor of online violence at a time when there was even less support than there is now for those finding themselves in my situation, let alone a young Black woman with a confident voice. The poor response from society, law enforcement and other people in politics was to say:

'Bear with it.'
'It's part of the job, just ignore it.'
'This is what it's like to be a woman in public life.'

My story is just one in a sea of millions. This abuse is pervasive and happens in every corner of the internet, and yet there's little help for victims. Step one of solving this is to equip ourselves and those around us with knowledge and support, and to reimagine our experiences online and with each other – and this book aims to provide you with those tools.

The prevalence and impact of online abuse

Online abuse happens far more than it should. And far more often than a lot of people realize: almost half of internet users in the US have personally experienced online harassment, with 27 per cent reporting to have experienced severe forms such as physical threats, sexual harassment, stalking and sustained harassment. According to Amnesty International, it happens to a woman every thirty seconds on Twitter alone, and according to the United Nations, women globally are twenty-seven times more likely to be harassed online than men.

Online abuse towards women – which falls under the umbrella of online gender-based violence (OGBV), which also includes the violent experiences that non-binary, trans and intersex communities face – is an extension of the offline, and too often physical violence many women disproportionately face. But, sadly, the data is still limited. When experts talk about online violence, they are often narrowly focused on the cyberbullying of young people. It's as if somehow – magically – we develop superpowers and are no longer susceptible to online bullying after our eighteenth birthday. Or they use language that prioritizes a limited, masculine, heterosexual, white-privileged viewpoint, which both erases and 'others' the experiences of minoritized communities.

By letting these experts shape the conversations, we overlook forms of abuse that affect a diverse range of people, and totally bypass the nuance of their experiences. We end up ignoring Black women, who experience misogynoir (a combination of anti-Blackness and misogyny). We fail to understand what trans people feel when they face specific forms of abuse such as intentional misgendering and deadnaming. And those with disabilities are completely ignored in the development of new multimedia products on social media, like audio chat rooms, or having to witness people laughing at visible disabilities in viral memes or GIFs.

We also tend to see online abuse through the lens of celebrities, but by focusing on them we're glossing over the fact that online abuse affects everyday people and communities in much more insidious ways – people who don't have the resources or platform to find support and justice in the same way famous people can. Not to lessen the experiences of celebrities, but we have to recognize how this issue affects victims of all backgrounds, especially those with limited social and cultural capital. Which is why this book focuses on equipping the most marginalized in our communities – and making sure no one gets left behind.

My anger, my desire to make change, and my sometimes-helpful stubbornness in refusing to accept this as the status quo are why I set up Glitch. My goal is to end online abuse. I want to help knock down the barriers that prevent women and marginalized people from speaking their truth, engaging in debate and having the careers they desire. Glitch is a UK-based charity that raises awareness of the long-lasting effects of online abuse, advocating for systemic change and legislative reform, while empowering thousands of women and members of minoritized communities to navigate the online space happily and safely.

The COVID-19 pandemic only exacerbated the problem. As CEO of Glitch, and in partnership with the End Violence Against Women Coalition, I launched a nationwide survey – and the results, based on nearly five hundred responses, found that almost half (46 per cent) of respondents experienced online abuse during the first lockdown in 2020, and a third of these said the abuse was worse than in previous years. Black and minoritized women and non-binary people experienced higher levels of abuse, were more likely to change their behaviours as a result, and were more likely to feel their complaints to social media platforms were not adequately addressed.

A rise in online abuse is stifling freedom of expression and joy, and is causing harm on a mass scale. This book doesn't see or frame online abuse in opposition to freedom of expression, but rather believes that those who are disproportionately affected by online abuse deserve to have their human rights protected too.

Our online spaces are continually being hijacked and weaponized by bad actors, with technology reproducing and magnifying all the inequalities we see offline. And the impact? An exodus of women leaving the online space because they feel unsafe. A generation who knows the immense power of the internet, yet feels ill-equipped or hesitant to fully embrace it. People of marginalized genders who are told they must tolerate online abuse as it's 'simply part of the job'. Young girls who grow up to believe the internet's polarity and toxicity are normal. Parents who are fearful of their children being online, and loved ones who are confused about how to provide support and who might unintentionally victim-blame.

Alongside calling for long-term systemic change, as the founder of Glitch, I develop and deliver training programmes and workshops for women and non-binary people so they can stay safe online. This gives us useful intel and data on how people are navigating the online space, their experiences, the different forms of online abuse, and how tactics are evolving – enabling us to continue to advocate for change that will actually help.

All of the work the Glitch team and I have put in over the last few years has helped thousands of people around the world, as well as helping me to develop a go-to toolkit for digital self-care. But it has also been a stark reminder of how much work there is still to do in order to tackle online abuse. The message needs to be loud and clear: online abuse is never okay!

Why is this book needed?

So much has gone into highlighting the need to make women feel safe offline without putting the sole responsibility on their shoulders. We have been pushing back against victim-blaming language – the kind that says what a woman wears or drinks affects her validity as a victim. But online, we remain megabytes behind. Victims of online abuse are exactly that: victims. Rather than addressing the real problem – a tech culture that's fatally flawed – we're told we are the problem.

I want to stress that, although this book focuses on my experiences as a Black woman online – and although the majority of statistics available are based on cis middle-class women in the Global North – this does not at all negate the experiences of other minoritized groups. This book is for all marginalized genders (and allies). I hope the data presented in these pages, as well as the diverse experiences and wisdom recounted by experts from many backgrounds, will provide you with a small window into what being safe online means – and what it requires – for minoritized and multi-intersecting identities that are systemically oppressed in our society.

This book collates the lived experiences, advice and painful lessons I and some of my nearest and dearest have learned over the last ten years – from those in my global professional network to some of my closest friends at home. These include activists, founders of global and small NGOs, journalists, former politicians and fellow survivors. The hope is that, by sharing these insights, fewer people – especially women – will have to fear and endure the emotional, physical and sometimes financial turmoil of online abuse first-hand.

Introducing digital self-care

Through Glitch, I've been developing the system and frameworks I wish I'd had in those darkest moments of online abuse. This book gives me an opportunity to pass on essential resources and lessons to those who need them right now.

Digital self-care is about understanding the realities of the online world and the many consequences we're facing while we're currently being let down by the systems in place. We can't implement online boundaries if we don't know what we're defending ourselves from. We need this knowledge to equip, prepare, and set personal boundaries for ourselves – while also taking steps, both big and small, to make others' online experiences safer and more joyful too. Not to mention educating ourselves on how and why we should continue to hold tech companies and governments accountable. And, finally, digital self-care is a healthy way to address the aftermath of violence and trauma. A way to kick-start our healing and salvage our relationship with the online space.

Throughout this book, we'll dive into a range of topics related to digital self-care – such as digital citizenship and safety. For so long, women have been conditioned to serve others before ourselves: to put our own needs on the back burner while denying ourselves play, joy and self-expression. Digital self-care and self-defence is saying 'enough is enough'.

This book will help you to understand the different layers of online abuse and how they appear. When we can recognize perpetrators and their typical behaviours, we take back our agency. The purpose of this conversation isn't to make you feel shit, or depressed about the state of the world, or make you retreat offline. Quite the opposite. With the right knowledge and skills, you can gain confidence and experience joy, both online and offline.

How to use this book

The book is divided into two sections. In the first four chapters, we'll build our foundation of knowledge – understanding what online abuse is, recognizing its many forms and learning who the key player

Then we'll move on to your **digital self-care tooll**

actionable insights you can take with you into every single online experience moving forward. These include strategies to keep yourself happy and safe online, tips on stepping up your digital security, and advice on how to be a better digital ally in your online and offline communities. If you are currently experiencing online abuse or know someone who is, flip to Chapter Five for actionable advice you can use now.

The final chapter of this book discusses my own reflections, milestones and mistakes – these are included with the intention of transparency, and to help dismantle the rigid perfectionism that is an integral part of white supremacy culture. Not only does it force all of us to (over)work to impossible standards, it also makes us feel like we are never able to make a mistake. This is cancerous to feminist and liberation movements, and on an individual level it can lead to guilt, shame and eventual burnout. The last chapter captures an aspect of a very active journey I am on now and will always be on – unlearning. As Audre Lorde famously said: 'The master's tools will never dismantle the master's house.'

This book shouldn't need to exist. Tech companies could have eradicated much of the problem a decade ago. Instead they are reproducing and sometimes exacerbating the same inequalities, the same harms and the same biases we see offline. (The fact user safety wasn't a priority for the vast majority of tech creation is a whole other issue and another conversation.)

We're now at a tipping point. Year on year, we're seeing an increasing number of what I call 'glitches' online: violations of human rights, examples of gender inequality, and threats to democracy. Glitches that are preventing both the internet and us from fulfilling our potential.

Who is this book for?

If you're one of the millions of women who've already experienced online abuse (probably more than once, as statistics tell us), felt isolated and were forced to blame yourself, I hope this book provides some comfort. I hope you feel seen and heard and that the information in these pages equips your community to better support you. I hope you understand that what happened or is happening to you is 100 per cent wrong, and I hope that the digital self-care toolkit lessens the burden of knowing what you need to do next. I hope you'll pick this book up whenever you need a shoulder to cry on, or a pep talk and a strategy to get back online.

This book also seeks to be a helpful guide for anyone looking to support someone else. You could be a parent, teacher, sibling, employer, agent, publicist or friend who wants to know how you can be there for someone who is starting to build their online presence but is fearful, or someone going through online abuse. If you don't understand why they're still online, or why it's impacting them so much, this book will provide insights into what they're experiencing. It contains the wisdom, boundaries and commitment to self-care I wish I'd had at age twenty-seven when I first received online abuse. And how awesome would it be if some of you were also inspired to join the mission of tech accountability? If we don't all play our parts as digital citizens, our online spaces will continue to be used against us.

We all need to hold ourselves accountable. I'm no exception to this. One of the biggest lessons to learn is that the line between perpetrators and victims is often blurred. We need to be continuously mindful of who we speak to online and how we speak to them. We need to be more compassionate about how we use our platforms. How can we post with greater empathy for those on our platflorms? How should we respond when witnessing online abuse happening to someone else? How can we better shape social norms, both online and offline? How can we *all* become better digital citizens?

Reversing the prevalence and damage of violence online will take a collective effort, and far more than this book can achieve on its own. But I hope that the following pages will make you think more about what we can all be doing every day to make our online spaces safer. I also encourage you to share your learnings with those closest to you. Opening up and having these conversations is how we can slowly build up our armour and defend ourselves and others against online abuse as a wider society.

Our online communities require as much attention and care as our offline ones do. As digital citizens, it is our responsibility to **be the change we want to see**.

So let's get started.

Chapter One: Why this book shouldn't need to exist

The developers of these apps are well rested billionaires who participate in the leisure life. We arguing with strangers on here and the rent still due.

The Nap Ministry, Twitter, August 2021

One of my biggest pet peeves is victim-blaming language. Perhaps this stems from unresolved trauma that I need to add to my growing list of 'topics to take to therapy'. But phrases like 'Don't feed the trolls' and 'Just ignore it' are irritating and so incredibly unhelpful.

On Christmas Eve in 2018, I was reporting an online stalker to the police shortly after publishing an article about Meghan Markle and – ironically – online abuse. Do you know what the officer then said to me? 'Well, if you made your account private and didn't write these things, this wouldn't happen.' Um, thanks?!

It saddens me, because it absolves the people in power of actually having to do anything. All the responsibility is piled on women and other vulnerable people to make themselves safe and avoid online abuse. Which is bollocks. I'd bet you my entire collection of Adele merchandise that even the most careful women minding their own business are still abused. Black, bold, proud women being themselves are forced to battle an onslaught of abuse just because of their profile pictures. New mothers posting about their experiences of motherhood on forums or even on their own social media accounts have been painfully attacked. Women can post on almost any topic – animal rights, climate change, healthcare – and abuse usually follows.

As a result, women are 'advised' not to talk about controversial topics. At best that's a subjective and unhelpful piece of advice that means we are apparently supposed to avoid talking about bodily autonomy, period equity or the gender pay gap. Yet a man can discuss these things on social media and be adored and avoid the abusive terrain women have to traverse. At worst, this 'advice' is a heteronormative silencing tool around the topics of the liberation of marginalized communities and social justice. And any topic discussed as *insert minoritized identity* is seen as controversial by virtue of the person being from *insert minoritized community*. This isn't right, but it is the reality and it's why this book is needed.

It's time we start countering this narrative that it's a woman's fault she's experiencing online abuse. Or a trans person's. Or a disabled person's. It's not the victim's fault, and it's also not their sole responsibility to make the necessary changes to eradicate the abuse. It's **everyone's** responsibility.

Offline and online abuse

I'm not anti-tech. To be honest, it's sexist framing to call passionate women campaigners 'tech naysayers'. It's an old tactic, and it's getting boring.

Ever since the 2000s, I've always been a big lover of the internet and new tech. The passion I – and others like me – have for the potential of the internet is why we do what we do. Just think about all the good it can accomplish. The people we can connect with around the world. The lessons we can learn from some seemingly random blogger or vlogger. How we can educate ourselves and learn new terms and even entire languages. The new careers we can pursue. All through the World Wide Web. Many people have even found love and companionship there. It's how I met my boyfriend – through the dating app Hinge. Social media alone has allowed me to make a positive impact on others, and them on me.

But for all the good it has provided us, the internet has also brought a mountain of avoidable harms. And that's because it doesn't exist in a vacuum. What we see happening online is a continuation of offline violence, and if you follow this path it almost always leads back to the patriarchy. We live in a patriarchal, heteronormative world – so how can we expect the internet to be any different? It's impossible to separate OGBV from its offline counterpart, as each feeds into the other. The systems that currently hold women down offline don't magically disappear online; the shadow of the patriarchy hangs over the digital space too. Racism and white supremacy, homophobia, transphobia, ableism and all other forms of bigotry exist as part of a continuum that exists both online and offline.

So, while I love technology, if we're going to talk about online safety and accountability, we're also going to have to acknowledge the offline conditions exacerbating the problem. Part of it is a lack of education about the systemic issues that affect us. Relationship and sex education (RSE) was only recently made mandatory in the UK but is key to teaching teenagers what healthy, respectful, consensual relationships are, and what crosses the line into the inappropriate. Our political education is compromised by our heavily colonized curriculums. And there's a real absence of open, transparent dialogue surrounding racism, sexism and other examples of systemic oppression. These offline educational shortcomings all contribute to what we see and experience online, and this is why they're so important to be aware of.

Similarly, OGBV is inseparable from the rights of women and those outside the gender binary. What we're seeing play out online is nothing new. Historically, our rights have always lacked the attention, care, investment and resources they deserve. Governments aren't investing enough in programmes and services to combat gender-based violence, and we don't have the laws and policies needed to support anti-discrimination efforts offline. This means online platforms are left to replicate the problems we've seen and heard offline a million times over.

I spoke to Hera Hussain, founder of Chayn – an online volunteer community that creates intersectional and multilingual resources for survivors of gender-based violence globally, and works to improve the online experience of those seeking support. She put it simply: 'We're all victims of the same issue. Even the perpetrators themselves are victims of patriarchy. Because people aren't born with the textbook of toxic masculinity and rape culture. We absorb it from the environment and we pass it around in our interactions with people. We're all victims of patriarchy and that's why it's so endemic and hard to spot. And then when you start unravelling the different threads, it pops up in the most unexpected places, as well as the most obvious ones.'

What I do think is avoidable is the scale at which we're seeing harms occur across the globe. Abusive content can easily be shared across platforms, allowing it to proliferate at speed and making it difficult to contain. It's the reach, speed, amplification and permanence of abusive content online that makes it distinct from offline abuse.

Laura Bates, writer and founder of the Everyday Sexism Project, explained how online spaces are the perfect home for all sorts of toxic and damaging behaviours and perspectives: 'Of course, people point out that the internet is revealing to us existing forms of hatred that have always been there. And I agree with that, I think that's true, but I also think that it doesn't only reflect back what's there, it also exacerbates it in a number of different ways. It provides ideal conditions for abuse that aren't available in the physical world. For example, a direct line to female public figures or politicians, where people can access them so much more easily. That's new. An echo chamber where people with already problematic views can be radic-alized very quickly and have their views confirmed and exacerbated by meeting a like-minded community in a way that wouldn't have been possible at such scale before.

'There's a deliberate radicalization and grooming of boys – teenage white boys, in particular – into forms of white supremacy and male supremacy, which they might not otherwise have encountered. The impunity exists online and normalizes, and therefore exacer-bates, these kinds of behaviours.'

A particular online group Laura referred to is incels. 'The incel community is the most violent corner of the so-called manosphere. It's a community devoted to violent hatred of women. A community that actively recruits members who might have very real problems and vulnerabilities, and tells them that women are the cause of all their woes. A community in whose name over a hundred people, mostly women, have been murdered or injured in the past ten years.'

In August 2021, Jake Davison killed five people in a mass shooting in Plymouth, Devon. Evidence points to him having been involved in various online misogynistic exchanges in the lead-up, including one with a sixteen-year-old girl a few days before.

The online space has become another tool in the belt for supremacists.

The reality of tech

Online violence and radicalization is one of the many defects of tech. We need to fix these glitches so the World Wide Web can reach its full potential. But, to do this, there are so many intricate layers to unpack and consider.

Everything I've mentioned up until now is the reality we live in. Governments and multibillion-dollar companies are letting us down. They aren't willing or able to do their part to significantly reduce online abuse and its impact. Most tech platforms weren't built with the safety of women in mind, and new platforms still fail to carry out a risk assessment of how they will be negatively used against minoritized communities.

The first version of Facebook, called FaceMash, was created by tech bros across the pond so college boys could rate the hotness of the women at their university. How can a later iteration of a platform designed for objectification ever hope to protect those it set out to marginalize? And another example: in 2021, Twitter rolled out Spaces, which alienated disabled communities. The new feature allowed users to create rooms where they could talk openly. But this attempt to create an environment for free-thinking paid little consideration to the deaf and hard of hearing. So much of Twitter's video content is already uncaptioned, making this opportunity to right the ship an obvious one. Yet those communities were left out of Spaces too.

These are just two examples showing who is – and more importantly, who isn't – considered when designing platforms. The idea that online platforms are neutral is a fairy tale. It's not a few bad apples ruining the experience for the rest of us. The very DNA of these platforms is in conflict with the best interests of a large number of their users.

Azmina Dhrodia is a leading expert working at the intersection of human rights and women's equality online. She explained her viewpoint: 'When women speak out online and receive threats of violence or abusive comments as a result, and when that abuse isn't dealt with adequately or consistently by platforms, it can have a silencing and censoring impact on how women use their voices in these online spaces. Focusing on women is not to deny the experience of abuse men also get online, but we need to talk about the very gendered element of online abuse that's rooted in structural discrimination, and patriarchy that we see manifest in online spaces.'

-en and girls across the globe are walking on eggshells of the fear of online abuse. Research by Plan International found that 43 per cent of girls aged 11–18 admitted to holding back their opinions on social media for fear of being criticized. This is not only having a devastating impact on mental health and well-being, it's also a violation of human rights and is eroding our democratic engagement. If young women do not feel they can speak their mind, and cannot take part in democracy, there's something seriously wrong with society.

These young women censoring themselves, or not thinking tech is for them, creates its own glass ceiling. It's just another barrier they have to smash past, ensuring poor representation across sectors and careers. It forces them to ask themselves, 'Why would I want to run/build/speak?' – because they know that, when they do, it's death threats, sexual harassment and racist slurs. As a result, not only are women silencing themselves, they're leaving online platforms altogether.

If you aren't familiar with the feeling, put yourself in their shoes. Would you want to be in a space like this, putting yourself in a vulnerable position, as a young person? I would imagine not. People that want to make the world better shouldn't have to face the fear of violence when leaving their mark.

Why running away isn't a solution

When people say victims should remove themselves from platforms after suffering abuse, they overlook all those who can't. As Hera Hussain shared with me: 'When we talk about the online space being unsafe, we often miss the fact that there are so many people in communities whose offline world is unsafe. They might not have support from their family. There are countries with laws that think their sexuality is illegal. They might be surrounded by so much negativity but can make those online spaces their own. They can set up those gardens of hope. They can create new communities or family support networks. They can build online profiles. They can create platforms. They can earn money. They can feel validated.'

A lot of people enter the online space because they've been ostracized offline. Disabled people, for example, can come to rely on online communities if it is difficult for them to develop relationships in person. For LGBTQIA+ individuals coming from homophobic families, communities or cultures, online spaces – in theory – can provide a much-needed escape from oppressive, abusive offline environments. And we all experienced an increased reliance on online communities during the 2020 and 2021 COVID-19 lockdowns. As an alternative to face-to-face meetings, we took to the internet to stay connected.

If we want to make a difference, we need tech companies to improve policies and rethink their approach in order to keep every-one safe – Black, white, Asian, LGBTQIA+, non-binary, man, woman . . . The next generation of tech innovators needs to be encouraged not to break things fast and apologize later, but rather to create tech that's truly disruptive and tackles issues of online inclu-sivity. And they should do this because they truly care, not because they want to further their billions for some CSR (corporate social responsibility) box-ticking exercise.

However, these are long-term changes that, despite my and many others' wishes, won't happen overnight. And in the absence of systemic-level change – for now at least – we need to practise digital self-care so we can continue to utilize online spaces. Yes, it's frustrat-ing that the responsibility falls on those bearing the brunt of the abuse. But looking out for ourselves and our communities, while simultaneously pushing for the systemic change we need to see, is how we will eventually transform the online landscape for the bet-ter. We can't fight the good fight if we're burnt out, suffering from abuse and fearful of the online world. Digital self-care is how we build the stamina and equip ourselves with the tools we need to navigate the world online.

The absence of minoritized groups

I probably wouldn't be here talking about this very topic if it weren't for the few but mighty elders in the tech and gender rights spaces. Folks like South Africa-based Jan Moolman from the Association for Progressive Communications (APC)'s Women's Rights Programme, who took me under her wing several years ago and helped me channel my lived experience and a whole lot of anger into policy reform.

In a recent conversation with Jan, she brilliantly explained her thoughts: '[Tech] platforms are built with particular people in mind. And those people generally are white and have access and resources. The world is structured in a way that gives room to certain people and limits others. And this is the context in which technology is both produced and consumed. With online gender-based violence, we cannot have any conversation outside of the meta-discourse around women's rights, gender inequality and violence against women.'

Some of you will only face minimal versions of abuse, if you're 'fortunate' enough. But others will have a more sinister experience. In the early days of campaigning, I saw many conversations around online safety for children, which was brilliant. But I also wondered about the girls – how did their experience vary from the homogenous group 'children'? After all, girls will be treated differently, even in ways that don't seem toxic. So it worries me that when talking about digital rights – essentially human rights and freedoms in the digital age – we often overlook an extremely important human right: gender equality.

We deserve equality in the online space. But we're not seeing equality. We know from the statistics that women in public life are particularly and disproportionately impacted by online violence. As a 'recovering' politician since leaving office in 2018, this is a topic close to my heart. We can't on the one hand tell women to get into politics and on the other remain silent about yet another dangerous and life-threatening barrier. Particularly after the murder of British member of parliament Jo Cox in 2016 by a right-wing terrorist whose obsession with Nazis and white supremacy grew online. We must also acknowledge the enormous levels of online abuse Britain's first-ever Black female Member of Parliament Diane Abbott faces every day.

Proximity to resources – in other words, privilege – has been overlooked in many UK and European discussions on digital rights. Breaking this down further, when the rare opportunity to spotlight online abuse does occur, it's usually white, middle-class women who are able to gain media attention. That's something else I've noticed: Black and other minority stories were (and are) missing from the discourse.

Azmina Dhrodia shared a similar perspective: 'When you're a woman of colour and have yourself experienced intersectional discrimination in society, it impacts how you view the world. I see this issue with my eyes and my lens of being a woman of colour in online and offline spaces. And I wanted to make sure that when people are talking about online abuse, we hear different stories from different people to understand the different impacts.'

In the digital rights space, there is a huge range of women not even mentioned – those from different racial and religious backgrounds, communities who are falling through the gaps. This book exists to help end the erasure of our pain and our experiences. For all of us, but especially Black women.

Everyone in the digital rights space needs to be talking precisely, and helping to equip all women in politics, campaigning, journalism, blogging, sports and entertainment – not just white women. We need to look through an inclusive lens when we're tackling online abuse, so people aren't being left behind.

The importance of listening to Black women

For so long, Black women have been facing horrific online abuse and violence. But their cries for action have gone ignored. In a *Wired* article in January 2021, researcher and writer Sydette Harry wrote about how tech companies don't listen to Black women: 'Harmful behavior toward Black women isn't enough to inspire change until others are harmed . . . making Black women visible as people is one innovation that tech can't seem to manage. It's one it can no longer avoid.'

Rachelle Hampton has written in *Slate* about Black feminists who were not only targeted by alt-right trolls on Twitter, but who successfully campaigned against them but were ignored: 'Before Gamergate, before the 2016 election, they launched a campaign against Twitter trolls masquerading as women of color. If only more people had paid attention.' Ashley Reese, senior reporter at Jezebel, said: 'Whether it was white men masquerading as Black people or other racist and sexist harassment campaigns, Black women have often been the early targets of coordinated harassment and doxxing before it spreads to other people of color and white people. Yet they've been largely ignored.'

Former journalist Michelle Ferrier founded TrollBusters – a rescue service for women journalists – in 2015, as a response to the online misogyny that went unaddressed by Twitter and Facebook. Michelle herself used to receive racist and misogynistic hate mail and death threats in the early 2000s, simply for writing her lifestyle column in the local paper. She even had police patrolling her neighbourhood. She eventually had to quit her job, in order to protect her family and young children.

Activists in the Global South have been campaigning about online gender-based violence and tech abuse since the 1990s. Some were even raising alarm bells when emails and SMS first became widely used. Glitch and I wouldn't be here if it weren't for activists in Latin America and across the continent of Africa, who challenged some of my white-supremacy conditioning. For this I will always be grateful.

All of this is to say that a **lot** of Black women have been shouting from the rooftops about this issue for not just years but decades. The writing has been on the wall for some time, but some have turned a blind eye to it. The truth is, online abuse has only become an issue since it began to affect the Global North. Specifically white middle-class women, and some men. But tech, governments, philanthropists, the media, the police and civil society all need to listen to and start centring Black women's experiences online when shaping policies and legislation.

Are we desensitized?

The 'sticks and stones may break my bones' philosophy we used to chant in the playground has become the approach many take when it comes to online abuse. It's difficult for those who have never experienced this abuse first-hand to understand how words online can have such an impact on someone. Especially on those in minoritized groups. And when online violence becomes a daily occurrence, victims – and wider society – begin to normalize their abuse, and can even come to expect it.

I spoke about this with Jac sm Kee – a feminist tech activist from Malaysia who works at the intersection of technology and power, exploring how tech influences all aspects of our lives. She told me: '[As a woman], you've been conditioned to think that because this is what celebrities have been going through, that this is normal behaviour. It's part of the job of being a woman online. Being a blogger, being a politician, being a campaigner.'

Online violence is an act so many of us are desensitized to. But we're only normalizing it further by dismissing our own experiences, whether as victims or bystanders. Jac says there is one simple thing we can do to help counter this: call abuse exactly what it is. Violence. I agree with Jac – we need to resist diluting how bad online abuse is and avoid comparison with other forms of violence. We don't need to see blood or bruises for something to be considered abuse offline, and the same applies online.

But for us to defend ourselves and our loved ones against online abuse, we first need to know what it is and to fully understand it. We need to comprehend that we're all different, and that online abuse can affect us in many ways. So let's explore what online abuse looks like so we can create effective boundaries and strategies. Let's name our monster, and start building our self-care toolkit.

I'd like to start by sharing my own story.

Chapter Two: My story – one of millions more

I wish I'd had this toolkit in the 2000s, when I was on messaging forums and sites such as Myspace, Hi5 and Bebo. I'm part of the generation that grew up with the internet and rapid tech advancement. Painstakingly waiting while the creamy-white Dell Windows 98 PC with the big hardware sleepily came to life and the AOL dial-up did its thing. Changing my MSN status daily to a UK grime lyric or an indirect comment to get a boy's attention. I would wait hours for the latest wifey riddim to download from LimeWire (we all did it – no judgements) or for someone to send me the latest hit via Myspace or MSN. It certainly wasn't as slick as using Apple Music or Spotify now. There were times I was home alone – my mum was out trying to make ends meet, and my dad wasn't around – so the computer was my outlet. I adored all of it. The World Wide Web was my friend. It was my connection to the rest of the world, all while in a small council flat in East London. But I do cringe when thinking back to some of what I used to say and share, the people I met, the MSN boyfriends I agreed to go out with. God knows how many of the strangers on the internet that asked me 'ASL?' (age, sex, location) were really who they said they were.

These joys of the internet are something I think a lot of us can relate to. Writer and presenter Yassmin Abdel-Magied agrees: 'I found a community online from a super early age. There weren't many African people around while I was growing up. We were (according to my dad) the second Sudanese family in Brisbane. I grew up in a very homogenous, monocultural society. For me, going online was about discovering and gaining access to the world.

'I learned so much. The conversations around race and social justice I had access to online were worlds away from what I had around me physically. The online space was always a place that felt like home in a way. I felt I belonged, that I had rights, and I found myself invested. The relationships I created online were exciting and were very real to me.'

Funnily enough, though, despite my great love for online spaces, I was the last out of my friendship group to join new social media platforms like Facebook and Twitter. For some subconscious reason, I was suspicious and for the time being perfectly content with what I had, like trusty BlackBerry Messenger.

It wasn't until I stood in the Newham Youth Council election in autumn 2007 that social media became increasingly important to me. It was the only way I could get my voice and message out to the young people I was representing. I had finished secondary school; I didn't have hundreds of kids who would vote for me just because they knew me. So I had to go out of my way to connect with people, and that's where my 'political brand' on social media was born. At the time, I didn't use Twitter to talk about and share details of my personal life. That was more for Facebook, because the people on there were those I trusted – from my church community, or old school friends I knew offline.

After graduating from the London School of Economics and Political Science, I started a WordPress blog about education reform. Post-2010, there were significant local government and education cuts. Decisions were being made about young people – affecting myself and my community – with no consultation on what we thought. While they were there to advocate for us, we were not being properly represented, and nor were we part of the decision-making process. I remember thinking, 'How can they genuinely promote positive change on my behalf?' I wanted to give myself and my community a voice. At the time, I wasn't a confident writer (Seyi in 2012 would laugh hysterically if you told her she'd be writing a book a decade later), so writing blogs not only allowed me to develop as an education policy expert, but also allowed me to hone my writing style. I began strengthening my core beliefs, and found a community online who had similar interests. My niche blog grew and found its place within a tribe of people who agreed with – or could have great and respectful debates about – education policy and the need for reform.

Through my platforms, my career slowly developed, and I eventually landed an international internship in Brussels thanks to my Twitter account. It was an eye-opening experience working within the European Union institutions, but after a while I felt so far removed from the communities we were advocating for. We claimed to be making 'life-changing' decisions about young people across Europe. But I remember wondering to myself: 'How do we know if these policy recommendations are actually working for young people across the continent?'

My internship was ending, and the opportunity to stand as a local councillor came up. So, at twenty-two, after half a bottle of wine to calm the nerves and quiet the imposter syndrome, I applied to stand for the upcoming local council elections. I remember going back and forth between Brussels and London every other weekend, absolutely knackered from the daily grind. But after nine months of door knocking, campaigning, leafleting, talking to residents and **lots** of walking, they elected me as the youngest Black female councillor in Newham. It was an especially big deal for me, as it meant I would represent the area I grew up in.

Going to Europe

With most UK councillors being sixty, white and male, I can see why somebody like me seemed like a peculiar fit. The online space continued to be key in getting my core beliefs and perspectives out there, as well as to encourage other young Black women into politics and attempt to bring about systemic change. It wasn't a tactic the old guard were using quite as effectively. There were a lot of magazines and TV outlets wanting to speak to the young Black woman effecting change in politics. I was able to capitalize on the growing media interest to talk about key issues and share perspectives on topics that were often slipping under the radar.

My election sparked a lot of interest outside the UK too. The European Parliament in Strasbourg invited me to talk about ways to increase youth engagement in European democracy and politics. This was before the EU membership referendum, but sadly during the resurgence of neo-Nazism and fascism across Europe.

I felt like, 'Seyi who?' My only other job had been the Brussels internship. Looking back, I'd lived a fairly sheltered life up to that point. The one time I'd been abroad on my own outside of work was a girls' holiday to Egypt. So being invited by the European Parliament to stand up in Strasbourg and talk about my ideas was a huge deal.

After I presented my ideas to MEPs, I went along to a special hearing to talk about the refugee crisis across Europe. There were rumours there might be a protest, but I never could have imagined what happened next.

There was a Syrian refugee on the panel. It was a surreal moment; it was the first time I'd ever heard a refugee tell their own story. We all read and watch news stories, but it's so different when you hear a personal account in the flesh. I had goosebumps hearing his story of seeking refuge in Portugal.

I listened as he shared about not being able to see his mum and sister in months, all the dangers of life at home, and how he'd left Syria to build a better life. It was one of those moments where you're just so tuned in and captivated by every word.

Then, out of nowhere, there was this horrible sound bellowing through the quietness of the room. I quickly realized our speaker, this brave human being who was openly communicating his pain and experiences, was being heckled and booed by several members of the youth wing of the French Nationalist Party.

It was a shock at first. I couldn't believe the disrespect. As a Nigerian Brit myself, I was deeply empathic towards our speaker. I felt it was such an honour to be there and listen to this story. I couldn't comprehend the fact that people were disrespecting this guy's honesty. Before I knew it, I had put my hand up to make an intervention to the panel. I was given ninety seconds, and the big clock in the European Parliament's hemicycle began the countdown.

I had no premeditated plans or speech outline. It just came out naturally.

I encouraged attendees, especially the hecklers, to reflect on history. On why we have refugees and war-torn nations. On the legacy of colonialism that has terrorized countries for centuries. Waves of emotion and passion came over me, and I began advocating for reparations. For an acknowledgement of colonialism and the brutality that has devastated countries around the world. For an investment in restoring countries that were pillaged.

My speech was interrupted by the bellow of cheers from fellow audience members and boos from the obvious suspects. Ironically, one of the junior members of the French Nationalist Party previously hadn't appreciated being interrupted, calling for us to respect the 'principles of democracy', but he clearly didn't seem to respect those same principles now as he and his comrades rudely interrupted me. My response?

'Hello, Mr Lover of Democracy, can I speak?'

As if I were in a pantomime, they replied with more boos and howls. And I guess it was this next line that captured the attention of millions of people around the world: 'You can boo me all you like, baby!'

I continued my impassioned unplanned speech as the cheers and heckling continued. Then I took my cheeky bow and sat back down.

Going viral

In May of that year, I came back to London and thought nothing more of it. I returned to my relatively normal life of being a young councillor and working a full-time job. Five months later, the European Parliament invited me back to make another speech about social integration. I felt confident, more polished and experienced, and I was ready. When they promoted the event I'd be speaking at, they used a recording of the impromptu speech (it was more of a telling-off, to be honest!) on Facebook – and it was from there my speech went viral. This incident coincided with early global conversations around race. I mean, this was 2016, and it took us until 2020 to stop skirting around the issue and start talking about race equity and injustices head on. Within a week, the video had racked up hundreds of thousands of likes, views and shares across different social media platforms. My followers dramatically increased. If I can be totally honest, my thought, at twenty-six years old, was I'd made it: 'This is sick. I'm going viral, and for the right reasons.' I had strangers in my DMs on my personal and public Facebook pages. I was constantly being tagged on Instagram, and I was excited to get that Twitter blue tick.

It was a strange experience, because the video would go viral in waves on different platforms. People would download it, cut it, create new versions that others would also share, and the views continued to grow. My notifications would quieten down, then someone would find the video, post it on a different social networking site like Twitter, and the clip would go viral again. Then the same would happen on Instagram and Facebook, repeatedly. I had church aunties telling me they'd seen my video in their WhatsApp groups.

This was my first experience of how one simple upload creates a digital footprint that's impossible to erase. It takes one person to knock down the first domino and then it's unstoppable. This wasn't even something I'd planned, filmed or shared myself.

Victim blaming

And then we come to the part of my story from the start of this book. When I was simply trying to get a workout in before starting my day. It's amazing how quickly normality can all melt away. It was February 2017, and instead of exercising and smashing my New Year's resolution, I was watching a flood of abuse, sexist and racial slurs, and even death threats draining my battery minute by minute.

The panic set in quickly. Suddenly, I felt incredibly vulnerable and paranoid in somewhere that was previously such a safe space for me – both offline and online.

As a local councillor, I had a relationship with the local police team, and I contacted them in a daze. Even that was a surreal moment. How do you verbalize this situation – whatever it is – to someone else? I remember exactly what I said to him: 'It's Seyi from Forest Gate. This is going to sound weird, but something's happening.'

I explained how I was receiving all these notifications on my phone. I repeated some of the comments to him. He told me to get to the police station immediately. Still dazed, I rushed over in my sweaty gym gear and ended up spending hours in the station, waiting to make a statement and then recounting the whole situation out loud to the police. While I was sitting there, I scrolled through all the relentless notifications. They wouldn't stop. I even had to ask the officers to charge my phone, as they needed it for evidence. There I was, at the police station, not knowing what to do, what to say or who else to tell. I'd promised my mum I would do the food shopping, but there was no way I was going to tell her why I couldn't over a text or a call. I sat there worrying about the parking and stressing over all the plans I had made but couldn't get on with, because now I was at my local police station . . . just waiting.

I had never, ever experienced online abuse of this magnitude before. I'd never had to understand its impact. And it highlighted the very first stumbling block for protecting myself against it. Legally, we have very few rights in terms of online abuse.

The police didn't handle it with the best of care. When I made an official report, the officer asked me to print out all the abuse I'd been receiving. I produced this Yellow Pages-thick wedge of evidence ready for the next steps. I even remember the thud the paper made as it landed on the officer's desk. I was asked to go through every single one of the demeaning comments and threats – to relive them – with a highlighter, and rate how bad I thought the abuse to be on a scale of 1 to 10. Rehashing my trauma to decide if a comment wasn't that bad compared to some of the others. Did I deem being called a 'ni**a' worse than someone telling me what he wanted to do with my clit? Was telling me to go kill myself a 9 or a 10? To make matters worse, I was told that only the 7-to-10s would be considered for investigation.

Sadly, this was one of many visits to the police station, repeating and grading the abuse to help build a case to investigate. On one occasion, I was at home and the doorbell rang. It was the local police team, who did a full sweep around the building, looking for who knows what and checking I was okay. As a UK councillor, my address was public, so there was a genuine concern for my physical safety. That's when I realized how serious my situation was.

I'll never forget one of the hardest conversations during this experience – telling my mum. I asked her to sit down, looked her in the eyes, and watched as her face turned from confusion to sadness as she listened to me recount my morning at the gym. I told her about the racist abuse, the threats to my life, and what people were fantasizing about doing with my body parts. Without meaning to, she was my first source of victim blaming:

'What did you say to cause it?'
'What did you do to make it happen?'
'Can you take it down?'
'Can you tell them to stop?'

Don't get me wrong, I completely understood her natural reaction. She's a Nigerian mother from a different culture and has a polar opposite level of experience with technology. She didn't fully understand what had happened, just that her youngest daughter was under attack. That said, it was still unhelpful. To be victim-blamed is to be made to feel that what's happening to you is your fault.

Holding tech responsible

I don't think I really slept that night. I remember opening my eyes dozily after a restless nap and checking my phone. I felt I had to do something. So I composed a public message to Twitter, Facebook, YouTube and Google. 'I've never been called a ni**a in my life, yet I've been called it at least three times in the last 20 minutes over your platforms. Can you help me? What are you going to do about this?'

The platforms' responses? Absolute silence.

It pissed me off. I'd been a loyal and model user from the moment I set up my accounts. Yet, when I needed help, they all let me down. Their silence spoke volumes.

Calling an incident out and speaking openly about it was rare back in 2017. Those who did try to were ignored. But I had carved out my space in the public eye, meaning the post didn't go unnoticed. A journalist contacted me through Twitter to come into the studio to tell my story. Within twenty-four hours of being at the gym, I was on ITV's *London Tonight* talking about the ongoing abuse.

My automatic response was: 'This can't happen to another woman.' I didn't want to shy away from it and become part of the problem – encouraging young people into politics while suggesting they had to grin and bear it if online abuse happens to them.

After *London Tonight*, I campaigned for several weeks, attending interview after interview, striving to create change. Lyn Brown, my local MP for West Ham, was by my side trying to get to the root of the problem.

I love the story behind how Lyn became my mentor. When I received my GCSE certificates, she was the person handing them out and congratulating us. Knowing I wanted to be Britain's first Black female prime minister, my mum – and I love her for this – marched up to Lyn and confidently asked her when, not if, her daughter could do work experience with her. Subsequently, Lyn took me on as a mentee throughout my early years of activism and local politics.

I have the utmost respect for her, because as soon as she saw my tweet, she was on the case with her contact at Google to get in touch with their public policy team. Unsurprisingly, their default approach was to victim-blame. We were talking about the comments I was receiving on YouTube and my other channels, and their first advice was simply to make my account private. At that moment, I felt like I was a scorned infant. Why should I? I'd done nothing wrong. Why was I being silenced and punished?

'Luckily' for me, they were launching a beta version of a new You-Tube functionality that used machine learning to pick up negative words and phrases in comments to moderate them. It filtered them into a locked folder and, if I agreed with the comments, I could choose to let them appear on the feed. I loved the idea of it; I thought it sounded great. And, at first, it worked. But those intent on causing harm figured out ways to trick the system, such as misspelling abusive words to avoid the filter.

When I experienced my online abuse, so many around me weren't equipped to help. Concerned loved ones, colleagues and even strangers were just asking me, 'What can we do?' or 'What do you need?' Even the Labour Party, who I represented as a councillor, couldn't properly help me. I was met with the same question: 'What do you need?' I had to endure the emotional burden of teaching people, particularly those with privilege, how to be an ally online and offline.

I kid you not, I ended up writing my own solidarity statement from the local council I'd been a member of for two years, which went into the internal briefing to the whole council from the Mayor of Newham – and was also used for Newham Council's social media. I had to persuade and present a case for them to show their public solidarity. If I hadn't said anything, the local Labour Party was just going to ignore the fact that the most high-profile young Black woman they'd had in a long time, who they loved to engage when it made the party look great, was facing abuse. They were going to stay quiet – happy with me in my joy, but nowhere to be seen in my pain.

The aftermath

It was a complete whirlwind. Looking back, I realize I had no time to fully process the trauma properly. I didn't catch my breath long enough to understand what was happening to me, both psychologically and physiologically. Between the trauma itself, engaging with the police and the victim blaming from loved ones and colleagues, I was automatically thrust into activist mode.

This was all swirling in my mind when I was in the middle of launching Glitch less than eight weeks later – I was campaigning for online safety while dealing with my trauma and looking for justice. The ordeal had given me post-traumatic stress disorder (PTSD). Every time the phone would ring or a notification would ping, my body would go cold. I'd feel frozen and worried sick about what would happen when I looked at my screen. It took a while to get diagnosed, as my story was the first time my doctor had seen an incident like mine. Sadly, even the healthcare system is ill-equipped to deal with this type of trauma. They referred me for cognitive behavioural therapy (CBT) but then the mental health professional didn't know what to do either, as the situation was also new to her.

There are so many ways that our systems are outdated and no longer support our experiences in the modern world.

So much of my personal lived experience to this day has shown me that, as a society, we aren't even remotely ready to be having all the conversations we need to have regarding safety online. Outside of Lyn and the support I received online, there weren't many people with the power to make a change standing up and trying to do something different. There were people in my party perpetuating the victim-blaming mentality. Saying, 'That's what you get for not staying in your lane.' Those same people were also telling me I was too cocky going to Europe in the first place and I shouldn't have spoken up.

It was Councillor (eventually Mayor) Rokhsana Fiaz who paved the way, modelling online allyship by tweeting that she was standing with me against the abuse and reporting it to the platforms. Without needing to be told how she could help, she stood up for me when I needed it most. Lyn also continued to pool her resources and had got to the bottom of where the waves of abuse were coming from. After some digging, she found the original video had recently been posted on what looked like an Austrian neo-Nazi online forum. It was the first time I was forced to take a good look at what the internet truly was. Of course we talk about it being the 'World Wide Web', but we are still in our own online social bubbles. The revelation of where the abuse was coming from opened my eyes and I realized that the real rotten apples – institutional racism, the patriarchy – were on all of our doorsteps, in our homes, in our bedrooms, thanks to the internet.

The buzz around my story and the several appearances I made on TV to talk about the impact of online abuse kept me in the headspace of all that hate and negativity. Sharing my story over and over chipped away at me. I tried my best to rest, but it felt impossible.

The first positive turning point in the campaign came as the Crown Prosecution Service changed their guidelines in the summer of 2017. Now, any form of hate crime committed online would be treated as if it had happened offline. This was a huge deal.

I had failed miserably at switching off and separating myself from the experience, so instead I jumped straight back in. I went right back to thinking about everything that had happened so I could help facilitate change and prevent others from going through the same situation. I slipped into 'fight mode' again.

But just a few weeks later I couldn't face it any more. Campaigning was adding to my paranoia. I already couldn't sleep very well. I was stuck in a rut of hiding my pain behind my smile, because I had to pretend that everything was okay. I couldn't speak freely at home because I didn't want to worry my mum. I had nowhere I could truly let my guard down and be normal and feel safe. It was tiring. I felt drained.

I needed a break.

This level of exhaustion pushed me to understand the importance of digital self-care. It wasn't solely the constant hate that I found tiring; it was the intense feeling of helplessness. That I couldn't do anything about something I hadn't caused.

I needed to control my story. I needed to take back my agency.

Shortly after the incident at the leisure centre, I'd been preparing to hold space for hundreds of young people across Kuwait as a facilitator for the British Council. The night before our first event, I shared my story with James Edleston, my co-facilitator and former youth worker. At first, I was deeply embarrassed. I'd still not had a break since that day at the gym and, somewhere along the way, I'd internalized the idea that this incident was my fault. I joined the ranks and started to victim-blame myself. Somehow, I'd convinced myself that I had something to be ashamed of and that I should keep quiet. But James was so supportive.

When you air out a situation like this with other people – the *right* people – you realize how fucked up it truly is. To this day, speaking to James remains one of the most helpful conversations on my journey. Having someone affirming to me that what was happening was wrong, that it wasn't all in my head, that it wasn't my fault, gave me the push I so badly needed.

After working in Kuwait, I finally took time away to move towards healing. Even so, there are still situations that will take me back to that first frozen moment of fear I felt in the gym. Without warning, my fight mode kicks in, similar to an elastic band snapping back. As is the nature of the online world, people talk about events long after they first appear online. The media doesn't help either, as it's all geared to what's trending, creating a perpetual cycle. Every time the video of my speech in Strasbourg recirculates, racists become agitated by it and blow up my feed again.

In the summer of 2017, as I started to dedicate more time to the campaign and speak with journalists to raise awareness of my policy recommendations, there was a rise in online abuse, hate crimes and intolerance in the UK. The polarization of issues and communities online was deepening, causing a further increase in online abuse and violence (something that was happening offline too). It quickly became apparent that most people still weren't ready to have a proper conversation about online safety.

Around the same time, the Mayor of London, Sadiq Khan, launched the pilot programme for an 'Online Hate Crime Hub'. Five specially trained police officers, headed by a detective inspector, were tasked with investigating all forms of online hate crime. It was more focused on online extremism, but they deemed my case violent enough to meet the required criteria. I met with the detective inspector, who told me they intended to build a case around the hate I had received. It was only down to pure luck in terms of the timing and the investment in this specialism that the Met Police could take action.

But for it to be violent in nature, only the racially abusive hate could be considered. I couldn't pick out any comments relating solely to my gender as evidence; they could only prosecute on a piece of abuse that was clearly racist or racially aggravated. Any abuse about wanting to violently harm parts of my body was going to be ignored. In the eyes of the law, I am only Black, not a Black woman. There was, and still is today, nothing in English law that protects me from gender-based abuse online.

I felt somewhat cut in half. Part of me was on the pathway to getting justice, and the other half was being completely ignored. Dr Kimberlé Crenshaw coined the term 'intersectionality' for this very reason. Because you cannot just cut me in half. It's being a Black woman – a (beautiful and powerful) intersection of two identities – that not only provides me with unique lived experiences but also exposes me to new forms of oppression and discrimination. My legal ordeal birthed the absolute conviction I had when setting up Glitch: that when we talk about online abuse and its impact, we must do so through an intersectional lens. If those with multiple and intersecting identities cannot access justice, then the legal system has failed.

As a Black woman, I was also very aware of the inequity of my access to justice. People who look like me cannot go to the police for a raft of reasons. There are disproportionate levels of police brutality against Black communities. Worryingly low numbers of sexual assault and rape cases go to court and end in a conviction. We recently mourned the loss of Nicole Smallman and Bibaa Henry, who were murdered in North London – yet two Met Police officers were more than happy to share inappropriate photos of their bodies at the crime scene in a WhatsApp group. We also mourned Sarah Everard, murdered by an off-duty police officer who abused the authority his profession gave him by pretending to be on duty. He also had a history of swapping racist, sexist and homophobic WhatsApp messages with five other police officers. I've lost count of the number of women who tell me or the Glitch team that they tried to report a death or rape threat to the authorities – and that the police refused to file a report because of the paperwork, instead giving terrible, victim-blaming advice masked as online safety. 'Just come off social media,' they say.

The bureaucracy involved in reporting my situation was ridiculous. If you put up a video that breaches copyright because you used someone else's music, social media companies will rip the video down in minutes. It happens to me often, as I post videos from dance classes. The speed at which they block my dance video from certain countries or remove it altogether amazes me. Once, my Twitter account was suspended until I deleted some harmless dance class videos with nineties R&B.

But when it comes to death threats, you have to go through a series of reporting tools. The police have to complete pages of data-request forms per platform to access information, and even then their requests may be denied. The paperwork the officers had to go through in my case was unbelievable. How are we supposed to get justice when our right not to be abused is in conflict with data privacy rights? When only parts of our identity are recognized in law? How are women and members of minoritized communities supposed to report online abuse if they're not going to be believed – and are often re-traumatized?

We need to fix these glitches in the justice system through legislation reform and police training, so victims don't slip through the net any more. It was through the formation of Glitch that I began to learn and identify what needed to change. I'd had no intention of becoming the CEO of a charity by the age of twenty-eight. I'd never imagined myself trying to bend the minds of some of the biggest tech platforms of the twenty-first century, or sitting on the safety councils of some of these global tech giants, or relentlessly researching how online gender-based violence manifests in different ways.

After a series of powerful learning experiences, I set my sights on becoming an advocate for system-level change. I realized we need a multidimensional approach – addressing both government and tech, but galvanizing individual digital citizens too.

Chapter Three: How to define
online abuse

Words scar. Rumours destroy. Bullies kill.

Zahra Sajwani

'Online violence', 'cyber abuse', 'cyberviolence' and 'ICT-facilitated abuse' are all terms used around the world to describe the phenomenon of negative and oppressive human behaviour online. But I've found 'online abuse' to be a more palatable term for the masses. Choosing one term can be tricky when it has to cover so much. In some instances, the abuse is targeted and sustained against an individual with an intent to cause alarm or distress. Alternatively, individuals can experience an onslaught of different, yet coordinated, forms of organized abuse in a short period of time – often referred to as a 'pile on', 'flaming' or 'mob attacks'. Abuse can be directed at individuals by people they know or by anonymous strangers.

When I first started Glitch, I used the term 'online violence', and our account was relentlessly trolled from all sides. Some found it offensive to describe online bullying as violent when people were being murdered or raped. Others just thought it was hyperbole. That wasn't what I wanted for Glitch – to be embroiled in online debates about the words in our mission statement – so, we simplified.

It was a painful lesson in finding a balance. One where you meet people where they're at, without feeling like you're compromising or diluting your language. Intentional language choices have become a huge part of my work for this reason.

The challenge of defining online abuse

How do we define online abuse if there isn't even a global consensus on what term to use, let alone what constitutes online abuse? I find it helpful to view 'online abuse' as an umbrella term for a plethora of tactics and harmful acts experienced by individuals online. Because new forms of online abuse develop so often, I'm not sure how helpful a long list of specific tactics can be for policy change or in educating the masses. For example, before writing this book, the term 'Zoom bombing' wasn't widely known – but that changed drastically when the COVID-19 pandemic began.

There's no way for legislation, schools or parents to keep up with the new trends in harmful behaviour. So I believe we need an umbrella term that covers all the tactics and acts people use to offend, ridicule or silence people – be it in a written, audio or video format – at the frequency and volume they typically come in. Acts that, offline, would be considered illegal. Where the sole purpose is to cause significant distress, serve as a threat or incite a fear of violence both physically and mentally. And it has to encapsulate the fact that what crosses that line is subjective – not everyone will tolerate online harassment at the same level.

When online abuse became mainstream

There's no one point where online abuse suddenly began to exist. Ever since the World Wide Web came to be, it has been there in some form – due to it being part of a continuum along with all our

41

problems offline. But the origins of present-day internet toxicity might be more identifiable. And while there were undoubtedly multiple catalysts, one particularly noteworthy incident was Gamergate.

Now, where to start with Gamergate. Some look at it as the seed of the rise of the 'alt-right'. Some might even argue that Donald Trump wouldn't have been President were it not for Gamergate. Either way, it's a textbook example of the division we see online today.

If you took a cursory glance at the issue when it first began in 2014, you might have thought it was about ethics in games journalism. That was the reason touted at the time, but at the heart of it was an insidious, sexist and anti-progressive counter-movement in online culture. The widespread trend of being 'anti-woke' or 'anti-SJW' (social justice warrior) can be traced in part back to here.

Gamergate started when accusations began to fly around that an independent game developer by the name of Zoë Quinn had started a relationship with a games journalist to get favourable reviews. The truth of the matter was that the source of the rumour was Zoë's ex-boyfriend, and the games journalist in question had no involvement in reviewing the game. There was no proof that Zoë had done anything unethical. Yet they were still subject to doxxing and threats of rape and murder.

Even though the idea that some ethical boundary had been crossed was unfounded, Gamergate supporters carried on regardless. Brianna Wu – another independent game developer who was outspoken against Gamergate – became a target and had her home address posted online. It got so bad that she hired staff to document all the threats she received, and she had to have personal security for events. Anita Sarkeesian also drew the ire of this crowd – her YouTube series *Tropes vs Women in Video Games* was already a popular target. She, too, was subjected to rape and death threats.

In the face of these accusations, many Gamergate supporters denied the harassment, claiming it was manufactured by the victims – a tactic often used. At the heart of it was a kind of cultural war over the fate of video games – though it was really about so much more. As with other forms of media, people were speaking up about the misogyny inherent in many games. They wanted more considered female characters. Gamergate was in opposition to this progressivism – its supporters were mostly disaffected young men who felt their space, their one 'safe' retreat, was being invaded.

It isn't hard to see the parallels between this and what led to the rise of Donald Trump. These were people who felt their voices were being quashed in favour of minoritized communities, rather than what was actually happening: that minoritized communities were finally able to speak. Nevertheless, it wasn't taken seriously, and now here we are.

What do other experts think?

One goal I had in writing this book was to gather together a wide range of perspectives and experiences. To do this, I interviewed several powerful voices in the space of digital rights and tech accountability. I found it incredibly useful to hear different experts define online abuse.

Azmina Dhrodia, who wrote Amnesty International's pioneering *#ToxicTwitter* report examining human rights abuses against women on Twitter, emphasized the myriad tactics and harms that are perpetrated against women online: 'They are deeply rooted in harmful, sexist and racist stereotypes. It's a unique component that women face versus men. Women are more likely to be attacked online for their physical appearance and have constant references made to their body. When they get threats of violence, it's not only death threats they're at risk of. It's often specifically the threat of sexual violence and rape.'

Echoing Azmina, Asha Allen – a digital rights activist based in Brussels who focuses on a Black, feminist perspective – said: 'It's the continuation of the offline abuse that we face as women from diverse backgrounds, as women from the LGBTQ community, as human beings. It's a manifestation of the continuous patriarchy; the misogynistic, sexist and racist society we live in. Online abuse is this manifestation at scale with rapidity. I know people try to minimize it in terms of the language they use: it's "jokes", it's "banter". Over-simplifying in this way speaks volumes as to how far in society we still have to go to tackle the issues that most countries, particularly in the West, claim to be past. They would say that they live in a post-racial society or post-colonial society. But we're nowhere near that yet.'

Psychologist Mamta Saha explained how she believes online abuse can happen: 'It can be subtle. A slow build-up of being stressed by being present online. It can chip away at you, to the point where that narrative of "I'm not enough" or "I'm going to get attacked" becomes part of your inner conversation with yourself.'

You don't need to experience a large-scale, violent barrage of abuse to feel the impacts of online violence. Online abuse is complex, and it's nuanced. The impacts can creep up on you unannounced, even if you might not consider yourself a direct victim.

No matter your own experience of online abuse, or which of the endless definitions out there you most relate to, working to build a greater understanding of what online abuse is, how it manifests in our daily lives and the common tactics involved helps us to recognize it in the moment.

The importance of intersectionality

Before we start to explore the common tactics of online abuse, I want to come back to something I mentioned previously – how online abuse can impact people differently.

In its most basic terms, intersectionality is the overlapping of social categorizations – such as race, gender, sexuality, age, class, education and gender identity – and how these can compound to create disadvantages and bring harm.

Intersectionality provides a helpful framework for recognizing the characteristics of abuse and harmful behaviour, as well as how people's level of risk and potential impacts will differ – requiring different interventions. It allows us to see how people's multiple identities, which add brilliant depth and colour to online and offline spaces, can also make them more vulnerable to harm. Not only does this enable us to see that abuse happens to particular people disproportionately, it also allows us to identify the sinister tactics that don't get enough media attention, and reveals how some groups of people may need to defend themselves accordingly.

For example, intersectional analysis helps us to see that older women are more likely to face email scams or rampant online misinformation, something which was prevalent during the 2020 pandemic. Research also shows that younger women and girls – as young as secondary school age – are having photographs shared without their consent or taken non-consensually and being publicly shamed on social media for it, despite it being wildly out of their control (and technically child pornography). A survey of children aged 13–17 by Childnet's Project deSHAME found that 25 per cent of respondents had witnessed young people secretly taking sexual images to share, while 10 per cent admitted to having done so themselves in the previous year. Meanwhile, trans women face challenges cis women won't, such as deadnaming.

Misogynoir – coined by Dr Moya Bailey – is an example of race and gender intersecting to create a particular form of abuse, harm and vulnerability, in this case specific to Black women. Asha Allen spoke to me about how Black women are disproportionately affected by online abuse: 'It's hugely gendered – particularly towards Black women. It's not only a way to silence them. It's not only a way to try and remove them from the online platforms. It's another way to constantly reinforce the fear that they live with every day. The fear of living in predominantly white societies that we manifest in our bodies every day. It's a continuation of that. You don't have to say this person is an N-word. You can just constantly minimize and harass someone in a way that makes them fearful of the society that they live in. Fearful to engage with it. And that is a continuation of white supremacy and the subjugation of Black women.'

Amnesty International's Troll Patrol project provides statistical evidence to support this lived experience. Looking at tweets relating to 778 women politicians and journalists in the UK, it found that 7.1 per cent were 'problematic' or 'abusive'. This amounted to 1.1 million tweets across the year – the equivalent of one every thirty seconds. And, from an intersectional perspective, women of colour were 34 per cent more likely to be mentioned in abusive or problematic tweets than white women. Black women were disproportionately targeted, being 84 per cent more likely than white women to be on the receiving end of abusive or problematic tweets.

Different forms of abuse can compound to create new ones. We need to stop seeing abuse as one-dimensional. We can be trans **and** Black. Disabled **and** Latino. A member of the LGBTQIA+ community **and** a woman. We shouldn't have to pick and choose which parts of ourselves are tolerable to bash and which we're allowed to be impacted by. It's all too easy to say certain abuse doesn't exist because we don't represent that particular type of victim. But because something doesn't exist in our world doesn't mean it doesn't happen elsewhere. Understanding the intersectional nature of abuse empowers us to let go of these dead beliefs and stop silencing or overlooking the pain of others. Standing up against **all** forms of oppression and abuse online.

Understanding how different tactics are used and their impacts enables us to look past the 'banter' and see the potential risks. Frankly, intersectionality is a critical and non-negotiable tool when understanding and addressing online abuse. Perceiving abuse through such a lens empowers us to make sure our online spaces are uplifting and safe for all people and identities. That the progress we seek and strive for is progress for the many, not just the privileged few.

Common tactics

Through years of research and listening to survivors from around the world and the stories they have to tell, I've collated a list of common online abuse tactics, though this is far from exhaustive as the list is forever changing. There are always sub-tactics that create new malicious behaviours.

You can find links to more information in the Resources section at the back of this book, under 'Understanding online abuse and tactics'. But there are some tactics I want to highlight here, so I can detail what they are, how they impact us and how they've affected the lives of their victims – some of whom are no longer with us.

Gender-based harassment

Gender-based harassment can involve the use of slurs, insults, profanity and often images and videos to communicate hostility towards someone simply because of their gender. This is how the Women's Media Center defines it in their Speech Project. The WMC was founded in 2005 by Jane Fonda, Robin Morgan and Gloria Steinem as a 'progressive, nonpartisan, nonprofit organization working to raise the visibility, viability and decision-making power of women and girls in media'. It also serves as a platform to ensure that women's 'stories are told and their voices are heard'.

Many harassers will resort to slurs such as 'bitch', 'slut', 'whore' or 'cunt', and include commentary on a woman's physical appearance.

Actress Alyssa Milano was subjected to reams of abuse after sharing a TikTok dance video she made for fun with her daughter. For me personally, this was such a sobering and sad story. I grew up watching her on *Charmed* on Living TV with my mum after school. So to see this person so publicly harassed was difficult. The trolls called her fat, said she looked pregnant, that she was too old, that she was an embarrassment and a bad mother. She's none of those. And the incident also showed how easy it is for anyone to find themselves in the middle of a gender harassment storm.

During the COVID-19 pandemic, we at Glitch produced *The Ripple Effect*: a report on online abuse and how it increased for women and non-binary people during 2020. In it, we found that 48 per cent of respondents reported suffering from online gender-based abuse during the first lockdown. So, whether you're on the receiving end of this abuse is basically a coin flip every time you post something.

Hate speech

What constitutes hate speech will vary depending on where you are in the world. Hate speech, both offline and online, is a criminal offence under European Union law. According to the Council of Europe's Committee of Ministers, hate speech covers 'all forms of expressions that spread, incite, promote or justify racial hatred, xenophobia, antisemitism, Islamophobia, anti-Black or other forms of hatred based on intolerance'. In the UK, there are specific laws that prohibit people from expressing threatening or abusive hatred towards a person based on their race, sexual orientation, disability, religion or gender identity. But take a trip across the Atlantic to the US – where many social media companies are based – and you'll find there is no hate speech exception to the First Amendment.

So, definitions will vary, as will ways of policing it. And, just like in my story, it doesn't always cover everything. UK legislation does not include gender-based abuse. Yet the Council of Europe holds a definition for sexist hate speech, which emphasizes expressions which 'spread, incite, promote, or justify hatred based on sex'. Typically, these are the rape, death and torture threats women and girls receive when they are subjected to the stereotypes enforced by rape culture and the patriarchy. Whether or not you can find justice depends on where you are in the world.

We still see shocking levels of hate speech online. In 2021, Glitch partnered with BT Sport to conduct research and develop a campaign around online racism in sports. It showed that a quarter of the UK population have witnessed racist abuse online, and 25 per cent of people who identify as gay or lesbian have experienced abuse. Meanwhile, 97 per cent of LGBTQIA+ young people have seen homophobic, biphobic or transphobic content on the internet, with 40 per cent being the target of such abuse. And online abuse of those with disabilities increased more than 50 per cent during the COVID-19 lockdowns.

The Pew Research Center found that, in the US, of the 41 per cent of adults who have experienced online abuse, 54 per cent and 47 per cent of Black and Hispanic victims respectively believe their harassment was because of their race.

The former MP for Liverpool Wavertree, Luciana Berger, has been outspoken about the extensive antisemitic abuse she has received online. Berger's abuse culminated in multiple convictions for her perpetrators. Yet, in 2020, the Community Security Trust recorded 1,668 antisemitic incidents in the UK. When compared to the 646 recorded in 2010, this highlights an alarming upwards trajectory.

When I spoke with Luciana, she talked about a particular incident. Hours after one of her abusers was convicted, a far-right website started a campaign against Luciana with the hashtag #FilthyJ*wBitch. It was just one of many. But because the website was hosted in the US, there was nothing she could do. 'I literally got thousands of messages over a number of months. It went into the winter of 2014, which was one of the darkest times. Over a three-day period alone, the police said I had over 2,500 messages across mostly Twitter, but also Instagram, my email inbox, you name it.'

Online hate speech can and has translated into the offline world. In 2018, Rachel Hatzipanagos, a writer for the *Washington Post*, published an article on this phenomenon, saying:

> *White-supremacist groups use social media as a tool to distribute their message, where they can incubate their hate online and allow it to spread. But when their rhetoric reaches certain people, the online messages can turn into real-life violence . . .*
>
> *White supremacist Wade Michael Page posted in online forums tied to hate before he went on to murder six people at a Sikh temple in Wisconsin in 2012. Prosecutors said Dylann Roof 'self-radicalized' online before he murdered nine people at a black church in South Carolina in 2015. Robert Bowers, accused of murdering 11 elderly worshipers at a Pennsylvania synagogue in October, had been active on Gab, a Twitter-like site used by white supremacists.*

Hate speech isn't 'just words'. It has a pervasive effect that seeps offline. And, as such, it should be treated with the thorough attention it deserves.

Cross-platform harassment

Being harassed on one platform is bad enough. But when that hate and vitriol follows you across the internet, it's called 'cross-platform harassment'. It can feel as if there's no escape. And it doesn't just happen on social media. It can spill over into the comment sections of articles, as well as emails, messaging services such as WhatsApp or iMessage, and even work channels such as Slack.

This is something Yassmin Abdel-Magied knows about all too well.

In 2017, she found herself on the Australian equivalent of *Question Time* – a hot-button-issue political panel show. 'It wasn't my first time, and I thought it was going to be a regular show,' she said. 'They put me up with one particular politician who had, at the time, expressed quite a lot of Islamophobic views. Behind the scenes, they told me they weren't going to bring up her comments about hijabs or burqas, but of course, they do. It goes all, "We should ban Muslims. We should ban anyone that follows Sharia law, blah, blah, blah." Naturally, I felt these people don't even know what they're talking about. So I give her a piece of my mind, in a way that's quite polite, really.'

The clip went viral. 'The original clip on Facebook got around twelve million views in three days. It gets translated into all these different languages. I get emails from the Netherlands, Iceland, everywhere. My social media was untouchable because of the amount of stuff coming through. Three days later, the mainstream media started going off on me. I remember seeing a huge picture of my face with some headline I don't even remember. But they accused me of "consulting" with terrorists, of being pro-FGM [female genital mutilation], profiting off taxpayers, all the usual rubbish. The rest of the press followed suit. I was on the front page of practically every paper, and the harassment went on for months.'

Imagine the impact of more than a dozen different types of notifications on a victim's mental health. What makes it even harder is that it's incredibly difficult to prevent or combat cross-platform harassment, which is in part exacerbated by the platforms themselves. While each will have its own ways of dealing with harassment, there's currently no way to report it as one incident.

Dogpiling

It's bad enough receiving hate from one person, but when a wave of people descend on you all at once? Cataclysmic. Dogpiling is an intentional, coordinated effort to bombard your social media with hate, distracting from your original message or any actual discussion. Often, allies can end up on the receiving end of online abuse themselves after trying to support someone else. Or, in the process of sticking up for a victim, they end up creating a counter-dogpile, derailing the conversation even further. Sadly, Glitch was on the receiving end of this tactic when we released *The Ripple Effect*.

The very nature of social media platforms has allowed harmful behaviours to thrive, with a lot of viral content going unchecked — whether the person featured in it likes it or not. And I'm not just referring to myself here. People who don't live in the public eye, those without a 'platform', can have a random tweet or TikTok go viral in a matter of hours. But that exhilarating rush fades away fast when your business suddenly becomes everyone else's.

Remember Rebecca Black and her song 'Friday'? If you were around in 2011, you couldn't escape 'the worst song ever'. Before that, she was a normal thirteen-year-old girl. Her parents were vets. They paid $4,000 for a music studio to produce the song and video for her, and in its first month it garnered about a thousand views. It was always meant to be a harmless pet project — something two loving parents did for their daughter.

Then it went viral. She became the target of the internet's vitriol, including fatphobic abuse. Rebecca had to be homeschooled while the FBI investigated death threats sent to her. She later wrote an essay titled 'What I Learned from Being a Target of Internet Hate at Age 13' in which she pointed out that's a stark and horrifying thing for anyone to have to experience, never mind a literal child. Given the lack of accountability online, way too many people felt comfortable bullying and harassing a teenager en masse.

Deadnaming

For many of us, our names are more than a name. They're our identity. Perhaps a name represents a connection to our families, reminding us of that aunt. Or maybe it references an artist who meant something to our parents. It's something that is uniquely ours.

Calling a transgender person by the name they went by prior to their transition is known as 'deadnaming'. Sometimes it happens by accident, but other times it is intentional. In the latter case, it is an insidious refusal to acknowledge that person's identity and is a form of direct harassment in which the target's former name is revealed against their wishes in order to inflict harm or hurt.

For the purposes of this book, I wanted to gather real people's stories for each of these common tactics. When it came to deadnaming, however, nobody got back to me. Not even to reject the request.

I think this speaks volumes in and of itself. It's such a difficult situation for anyone to experience, and sometimes even talking about a past experience can be painful and feel impossible to do. Talking about being deadnamed forces a trans person to keep reliving the trauma. It keeps them stuck in this cycle of reliving their past, instead of pushing forward with their lives.

Non-consensual photography, intimate image-based sexual abuse or revenge porn (*can lead to sextortion*)

Non-consensual photography, image-based sexual abuse and revenge porn are methods of distributing intimate images or videos that are taken with or without the consent of the victim, and then shared without permission. It can be an extension of intimate partner violence into online spaces. The images are either obtained by being physically involved, or by hacking into the victim's devices.

If you cast your mind back to 2017, you may remember when many celebrities had their private nudes leaked after an attack on iCloud accounts. Grossly dubbed by some as 'The Fappening' – which you do not want to know the etymology of – actress Jennifer

Lawrence was amongst the victims. In an interview on the *Hollywood Reporter*'s podcast at the time, she claimed it was 'so unbelievably violating that you can't even put into words' and that she felt 'gang-banged by the f*cking planet . . . You could be at a barbecue and someone could just pull it up on their phone.'

This is another tactic we saw a rise in during the pandemic. According to the Revenge Porn Helpline, there was a 22 per cent increase in reports in 2020 compared to the previous year. Two-thirds were from women, many from abusive relationships.

There isn't an agreement on the right term for this tactic. On one hand, there are those who don't want to associate any intimate moment with porn. While others – who tend to be pro-sex work and pro-pornography – don't mind the term 'revenge porn'. When delivering workshops internationally, I quickly learned the delicate balance of this terminology.

Doxxing (and other violations of privacy)

I'm sure many of us have been guilty of divulging a little too much information about ourselves on social media. But that's our choice. What happens when that decision is taken out of your hands?

Doxxing is the act of revealing information about a person without their consent, in order to victim-shame, to intimidate, for personal revenge and publicity, or to drive a public cause. Usually, these details have the potential to compromise their safety. Addresses, places of work, phone numbers, children's names and school information, pictures, financial details – these can all be leaked maliciously and used to ruin a person's life.

IT consultant Stephen Cooper has done research on some of the sinister uses of doxxing: 'the Anonymous movement and its associates on the 4chan message board are particularly keen on using doxxing as a way to punish enemies. 4chan has millions of members, and a hate campaign launched against a celebrity or company leader on that site can be very destructive. Mob attacks launched by 4chan include prank telephone calls, overwhelming amounts of abusive emails, network-swamping quantities of text messages and even physical attacks on the individual.'

You don't have to be a huge public figure to be a victim of doxxing, either. The number of outspoken women who have had their details leaked is astounding. Anna Merlan, a journalist who drew the attention of the lawless website 4chan after publishing a blog about them, saw the community publish her address and then plot what they would do to her. It started harmlessly enough, with pizza orders that were actually sent her way, but the discussion devolved into talk of rape and 'swatting' (see next page). They had her address, they had the means to affect her life, and the police couldn't or wouldn't do anything about it.

Having one too many pizzas delivered to your house is one thing; the FBI searching your home is another. That kind of fear is debilitating.

In my interview with Hera Hussain, she talked about a woman she knew who was doxxed and how this affected her life: 'People kept calling child services on her. Then the police would come to her house. And she's a Black woman in the US so . . . you know. It happened so much that she had to move home.' Home feels a lot less safe when people know where you live.

Another potential danger is when you're attacked based on untrue rumours or mistaken identity. In 2013, after the Boston Marathon bombing, Reddit users misidentified an innocent student, Sunil Tripathi, as a suspect. They were convinced they had found the culprit, partly because Tripathi had gone missing around the same time. His body was eventually found in Providence River and an autopsy revealed that he had died by suicide. There was no link between him and the bombing, yet his family had endured harassment and accusations of abetting a terrorist while they were desperately trying to find him.

Swatting

Named for the Special Weapons and Tactics (SWAT) teams in the US, swatting is the act of calling in a fake threat to the police – be it an active gunman or bomb – with the intention of having a heavily armed response team sent to a person's home. This has been a popular 'prank' to play on live streamers for some time. The victim is often completely oblivious, only knowing something's wrong when the officers bash down their door fully armed.

This tactic can be used with malicious intent to put someone in harm's way – or, at the very least, to disrupt their life. Not to mention the financial cost incurred by the law enforcement team breaking into their home.

What's especially insidious about it is how it can be triggered by something trivial – and how unsuspecting bystanders can become victims by chance. In one 2017 incident, a disagreement between two *Call of Duty* players over a $1.50 bet led to one swatting the other – who had given him a false address. This ended in tragedy when an unsuspecting twenty-eight-year-old victim walked out of his house to find out what all the commotion was about. He was shortly shot by armed police officers. The police had received a fake tip-off from one of the players that a person was holding hostages. The innocent twenty-eight-year-old, not at all involved in the dispute between the two players, left behind two children.

While not all swattings end in death, it's still a terrifying prospect. As with doxxing, perpetrators hold a lot of power over a victim by knowing where they live.

Online stalking

Put simply, this is taking the act of stalking online. But it's about more than following someone, even in a digital sense. It involves spying on them, researching and compiling every drop of information about them. It can mean communicating with them directly against their will, likely through as many channels and accounts as possible. They might not even know it's happening; someone could set up a catfishing account with the express purpose of getting closer to their victim.

This was a tactic used by Matthew Hardy, who admitted in a British court to having harassed women online for ten years. He would create fake social media accounts and post as his victims, who had no idea who he was or why he was targeting them. Hardy would steal pictures of them, pose as them to their family and friends online, and spread malicious lies about their sexual history.

The fact Hardy had no prior connection to the victims might be the scariest part of this story. For no reason at all, any of us could be the target of online stalking, which can have huge ramifications on the rest of our life.

Shock and grief trolling

Disturbingly, shock and grief trolling is targeting people with images or words the harasser knows will cause distress. This could be women who've had miscarriages, or anyone who has lost loved ones.

Feminist writer Lindy West was a target of Twitter trolls, who set up a profile posing as her recently deceased father, with the biography 'Embarrassed father of an idiot' and the location set as 'Dirt hole in Seattle'.

The *Great British Bake Off* presenter Matt Lucas faced something similar back in 2012. He temporarily left Twitter after a teenager posted a tweet making fun of his ex-partner's suicide. It cut Lucas deeply, and despite the teenager saying it was just a joke for his friends, it pushed the presenter to step away from the site.

Zoom bombing

Back in the peak of the COVID-19 pandemic and lockdown, when we were all battling Zoom fatigue from hours upon hours of looking at a screen, there was an influx of cases of 'Zoom bombing'. The term derives from photobombing, which is when someone makes sure they're in someone else's photo.

Zoom bombing is pretty much what it says on the tin: perpetrators break into online meetings. They might do something harmless enough. Some take it as an opportunity merely to be an annoying distraction – screaming and flailing across the screen. But it also has the potential to be much worse; others have used it to share pornography or explicit content non-consensually, in the hopes of causing distress to other users.

Researchers at Ryerson University's Infoscape Research Lab found that nearly 87 per cent of YouTube Zoom-bombing compilations contained racist, misogynist, homophobic or other objectionable content. Sadly, but unsurprisingly, a lot of this was directed against female teachers in online classrooms.

Gendered disinformation

Gendered disinformation is a specific kind of campaign aimed at undermining, attacking and discrediting women. It typically weaponizes hate, untrue rumours and outdated gender stereotypes to push the perpetrator's agenda. It's a particularly popular tactic to use against women in public life – politicians, journalists, activists and the like – though that's not to say it couldn't be used on anyone. It pours water on any passion a woman might have, with the goal of shutting down her freedom of expression and political participation online.

It might take the form of a fake nude image, or calling someone a liar for speaking out against harassment, or portraying them as a 'traitor' or a 'threat' to the stability or safety of a country. These baseless accusations are themselves a threat to democracies around the world, and are an ever-increasing feature of online politics.

There are three components that make up gendered disinformation: falsehood, bad intent and coordination. In that sense, it goes beyond your regular troll comment into something much more calculated and spiteful. And the abuse is often intersectional, with comments attacking a victim's gender and race, sexuality or religion.

The impact of online abuse

Hera Hussain shared with me why she believes online abuse has such a pervasive, deep impact: '[It] is such a powerful tool for abusers because you can physically leave a space, but your digital devices stay with you. So it's a way of making that abuse insidious. It's literally inside your house, your bag, your pockets. It stays with you. You can't leave that device alone. That's what makes it pretty powerful.'

Those who dismiss the idea of online abuse being violence will fail to see the full impact it can have. It can affect us in multiple ways. Yes, it is a psychological and emotional attack that affects our mental health, and equally it can hit us physically and financially, not to mention how this can boil over and impact our loved ones – and even human rights as a whole.

Physical impact

Aside from the very real threat of in-person, physical harm that can accompany online abuse, experiencing it first-hand through a screen can wreak havoc on your body and physical health.

A lot of this is linked to the body's stress response.

As psychologist Mamta Saha explained: 'Fight-or-flight mode flushes your brain with the stress hormone cortisol and leaves you stressed for so long, to the point where it becomes a part of how you operate. The framework of how you perceive the world becomes the way you take in information from the world.'

It's not healthy for any of us to live within our stress response for too long. It can be taxing on the heart. The increase in blood pressure and heart rate when you're experiencing or even anticipating an attack could lead to hypertension or increase your risk of a heart attack. It is also connected to gastrointestinal issues, and can worsen upset stomachs, abdominal pain or IBS. You might suffer from lower-quality or more infrequent sleep, leaving your body unable to adequately rest or recover. Stress also weakens your immune system, leaving you more susceptible to illness.

Psychological and emotional impact

In May 2012, an article titled 'Social Media and Suicide: A Public Health Perspective' was published in the *American Journal of Public Health*. The opening gambit was: 'There is increasing evidence that the Internet and social media can influence suicide-related behavior. Important questions are whether this influence poses a significant risk to the public and how public health approaches might be used to address the issue.' Online abuse **is** real, and online abuse **does** cause genuine harm. And we are all at **significant risk** of falling victim to it.

The psychological and emotional impact of online abuse is considerable. And the consequences run deep. When a victim's mental health starts to erode, it can lead to increased stress, self-harm, anxiety and even suicide.

Perpetual anxiety and stress – which might be accompanied by an inability to concentrate, do your work or live your daily life – can quickly feel all-consuming and overwhelming. When you receive a threat of violence online, especially if it's from someone anonymous, you have no idea if that threat will transpire in the offline world. And this leaves you in a sort of limbo, helpless as to where to turn or go next. Socially, you may start to feel withdrawn or actively isolate yourself from your community, which only exacerbates your inner turmoil.

Unsurprisingly, anger and anxiety were the most frequently

experienced emotions when facing online abuse. The *Ripple Effect* report found that 73 per cent of respondents felt angry and 69 per cent were anxious following incidents of online abuse. Black and minoritized respondents were slightly more likely to report feeling anxious than white respondents: 70 per cent compared to 67 per cent.

Research by Amnesty International revealed that over half of women who experienced online abuse or harassment suffered stress, anxiety or panic attacks following it. And 67 per cent felt apprehensive when thinking about using social media again. The experience of online abuse led the majority of respondents to modify their behaviour online and adopt defensive mechanisms to avoid experiencing abuse in the future: 87.5 per cent of Black and minoritized respondents said they had modified their behaviour online following incidents of online abuse, compared to 72 per cent of white respondents.

The impact is extremely personal. You feel trapped. Your mind plays tricks on you as you tell yourself you're exaggerating or that you probably deserved it. It is also a drip effect. There is one incident. And then another. And then another. And it compounds. Eventually, it feels suffocating.

Sometimes the crushing feeling from online abuse follows you to your work and shuts you out of it. You don't know who you can tell, so you suffer in silence. It's isolating. You don't want to tell your boss because you don't know how they'll react. What if they take your job away from you? This real risk to your income spirals, adding to the impact on your mental health.

Online trolls could be anyone. You may begin to question your partner, your neighbour, your friend. Until, eventually, you feel you're alone with no way out.

Online abuse pushes you into perpetual fight, freeze or flight mode. And living in this constant state of hypervigilance is incredibly unhealthy. Your fight-freeze-flight response is a gift designed to keep you safe from potential dangers in your surroundings. However, when the option of safety is removed from you – in the case of online abuse when the threats and dangers are relentless and all-consuming – your brain remains tapped into one of these exhausting modes. If the abuse doesn't quit, your defence responses won't either. All it takes is one tweet, one dogpile or one obscene text sharing more personal details than you feel comfortable with to push you over the edge.

Financial, professional and reputational impact

Online abuse – either experiencing it first-hand or witnessing it happen to someone else – can impact careers, leading to financial damage, reputational damage or a complete withdrawal from a chosen profession.

I've mentioned before the incredibly silencing effect of online abuse, particularly on Black women and minoritized groups. It's one of the reasons many women MPs choose not to run for re-election after facing or witnessing online attacks. And if we're already under-represented at the governmental and corporate levels, and online abuse continues to push women away from high-ranking positions, we're only going to be moving further from any hope of change.

It's an issue for many women in public life. If you're an influencer, activist, journalist or politician, these spaces are a part of your livelihood. You need to be online. So if you're unable to participate in these spaces properly, without fear of being bombarded with abuse every time you post or share content, that will have an adverse impact on your financial security – whether it stops you from being offered work, being paid for your sponsored content or causes your sudden withdrawal from your field.

It becomes your whole world, something Yassmin Abdel-Magied shared with me. After she faced online abuse following an appearance on TV, she started to see it reflect in her career: 'I had to give my phone away to somebody else because every time I opened my social media, my friends would notice my demeanour change completely . . . I've changed my phone number so many times I've lost count. I ended up moving house. I ended up losing all of my work. Even my local library cancelled an event because they were getting so much hate mail about me working with them. My life has never been the same since.'

Women who have businesses, particularly women of colour, are being driven from commercial online spaces by sexist and racist hate. And this has an all-encompassing, devastating effect on their careers and livelihoods.

There can also be the added financial burden of having to seek out mental health support from therapists or increase home security in response to threats. When I spoke with Gabby Jahanshahi-Edlin – founder of Bloody Good Period (BGP), a UK charity fighting for menstrual equity – about how she cultivates her predominantly offline life, we discussed the number of opportunities – or lack thereof – available as a result of no longer engaging with online spaces.

'Since I haven't been on Twitter or Instagram much at all, the opportunities don't come in the same way,' she said. 'The reality is that so much activist work, be it writing articles, public speaking or talking about your cause in interviews, is generated by a prolific online presence. But that presence comes at a cost to my mental health, and it's not sustainable to always have something new and interesting to say. If this is how I'm required to live to get this work, I don't want it.'

In May 2021, I did a match-day interview at Crystal Palace for BT Sport about the impact of online hate. As I scanned my mentions afterwards, my boyfriend had to stop me in my tracks. I was going straight past the positive and supportive comments, magnetized by all the horrible ones. I was actively looking for the bad. To this day, years after my first experience of online abuse, I remain teetered on a knife's edge and my fight-freeze-flight response is very easily triggered. After a public appearance, the notifications start coming in, and I automatically default to 'Okay, here we go', physically bracing myself, wondering, 'What am I going to see in my notifications now?'

We have to ask: why are we creating a culture that demands such a high tolerance for emotional pain in order for us to make a living? Why is the onus on women and minoritized communities to navigate this minefield in order to make money that anyone else doesn't have to struggle as much for?

Impact on family and friends

When we talk about the impact of abuse, typically we talk about the victim, the perpetrator and the environment. But we forget to consider the impact it can have on a victim's loved ones.

When I was part of Amnesty International's #ToxicTwitter campaign back in 2018, we encouraged people to speak out and write letters. People that I had never met would write to Jack Dorsey – the CEO of Twitter – on my behalf, and also wrote me letters of solidarity. I still have them. Some of them I will never forget. There was this one letter from a lady called 'Nana' that touched me differently. It was along the lines of: 'I'm a 70-year-old who has no interest in being on Twitter, but I know what it's like and how important this matter is because I had a young niece take her own life because of online abuse.'

In the early days of my abuse, I could no longer be myself around my mum, friends and loved ones. I didn't want them to worry, so I put on a brave face. When victims start to blame themselves, as they typically will in the current online climate, they isolate themselves from everyone they know and love. But, regardless of whether we let them in or not, those closest to us also feel the depths and impacts of our pain, and experience their own stress and anxiety – both over our direct safety and how best to support us and show up.

Azmina Dhrodia, women's rights campaigner, was sexually assaulted in Central London by a man who violently grabbed her crotch. After not getting through to the authorities, she confronted him, videoed him apologizing to her and posted her experience on Facebook. She then found herself falling victim to online hate and victim blaming. Then, prior to the release of Amnesty's *#ToxicTwitter* report, she and her family had to change their last name on social media platforms to preserve some anonymity and protect themselves against trolls.

'Before publishing the *#ToxicTwitter* report, I knew it was guaranteed to trigger some backlash, so I encouraged my family to change our surnames on social media platforms as it was unique,' she told me. 'I remember the conversation with my mum. I remember calling her and explaining that I was publishing a big report about women's experiences of abuse online and that people might target us online with hate as a result, and that she needs to change her name so she's not identifiable on Facebook. "Why would they target you? Why would they come after me?" she asked. She was just confused as to why anyone would come after her because of something I'd written for work.'

This is a stark reminder that an abuser won't just stick to their main target – a victim's family, partner, children and friends can all be directly impacted. Anyone connected to your online presence through mentions or pictures is fair game in the eyes of an abuser.

Impact on gender equality, human rights and democracy

Above and beyond negatively impacting our health and well-being, online abuse also stifles wider progress towards gender equality and is even a threat to human rights and democracy. Online violence carried out against politically active women is a direct barrier to women's freedom of speech and political participation.

The anti-democratic impact of psychological abuse and other forms of violence through digital technology is an undermining of a woman's sense of personal security, leading to self-censorship and even withdrawal from public discourse and correspondence. We begin to think ten times before posting something – having to decide whether or not we have the energy to deal with the trauma that may come with it. We begin to dilute our opinions to make ourselves more 'palatable' and reduce the risk of backlash, even though our perspectives *aren't* particularly controversial in the first place.

Often, the voices silenced in this way are the ones fighting for social justice. We already don't hear enough of these voices, and the abuse they receive means we're going to keep hearing even less.

The rapid development of tech has only exacerbated the problem over recent years, increasing the number of possible victims, magnifying the potential impacts tenfold and making it all too easy for perpetrators to stage attacks. As new platforms develop, those intent on harm continue to gain new weapons.

It only takes a few words to become terrified for your livelihood. And every case of online abuse has the potential to grow so violent that it can spin off into an offline attack. Think of the murder of British politician Jo Cox. **All off the back of online behaviour.**

In the huge majority of online abuse cases, you see a similar pattern for victims:

- Anxiety
- Fear of the unknown
- Feeling unsafe
- Being forced into some degree of self-censorship

All of these impacts are important and worth understanding when we discuss online abuse and what it means for victims and those engaging with online spaces. Also worth remembering is how different effects can combine and compound and this can have far-reaching consequences.

It's not as if you can receive one round of abuse, take some time and then you're fully recovered. Recovery is not a linear process and the emotional reverberations are long-lasting. The next time you read a derogatory comment, it's likely to sting you that much more (the drip effect), leading to deepening impacts and knock-on effects.

Not to mention if your experience of abuse isn't handled well by the institutions and systems that should be supporting you. Poor responses from tech platforms (or, more realistically, the lack of a response) can make a traumatic experience even worse – adding fuel to the fire of what already feels like a futile, isolating struggle.

What online abuse isn't . . .

Glitch consciously avoids specific language when describing experiences of online abuse. We refrain from using phrases such as the 'real world', 'virtual world' or 'in real life', as such terminology fails to acknowledge the blurred boundaries between our online and offline experiences – not to mention the complexity of the relationship between online abuse and offline impacts, and the growth of the metaverse. Using these terms can create a false dichotomy and a hierarchy of offences that often minimizes the impact of abuse when it takes place online.

There's something I want to make clear here: online abuse is not the same as debate or discussion. It is intentional harassment meant to silence and force vulnerable individuals and marginalized groups – particularly women of colour – to leave digital spaces. A lot of the time, it is an attempt to modify people's behaviour, such as forcing women to conform to a patriarchal society by pushing them into self-censorship.

Expressing an opinion online is not online abuse. Holding people to account for their mistakes, in and of itself, is also not online abuse.

Calling them racial slurs, sending rape threats and sharing an intimate video without consent all clearly cross the line into abuse. But I'm aware that not every situation is so clear-cut. The line between online abuse and calling for accountability is very often blurred.

Online abuse or accountability?

No one is perfect, we all make mistakes and it's healthy to learn from them. There's a lot of power in being able to ask yourself: 'Am I being called out here? Am I being held accountable for my behaviour and do I genuinely need to hear this despite it hurting?'

While online abuse and violence is very real, and should never be minimized, it's important to be honest with yourself and others. We can't start reporting and blocking anyone who tries to take us to task for wrongdoings we should be willingly holding our hands up and admitting to. Powerful movements can be watered down by fake news and outrage – people crying wolf about 'abuse' that isn't actually abuse can be detrimental to those who are suffering most.

However, taking the demand for accountability to the extreme is going to be a threat to any progress in ending online abuse. Is going back eight years on someone's feed to unearth racist or sexist tweets really achieving anything in terms of accountability? If you've had to search that far back, then there is a very significant possibility the person has changed. I would define the act of 'dragging up tweets' as public shaming, and there's scientific evidence that shaming achieves very little. Dr Brené Brown has done extensive research on shame and guilt, and asserts that 'shame is much more likely to be the source of destructive, hurtful behavior than the solution or cure'.

Maryam Hasnaa – founder of New Earth Mystery School and Resonance Apothecary – shared these words that have stayed with me: 'Are you actually holding people accountable, or are you just overwhelming their nervous system to the point where they go into dysregulation, compliance and virtue signalling? I don't know about you, but when I'm holding someone accountable, I want them to at least be in their body enough that they can make some real change happen that is actually sustainable.'

Actor, writer and advocate Jameela Jamil shared some takeaways from her own experiences online: 'I don't think the abuse was necessary. But I think being called out has made me a much better person online. While I think it could have been handled in a way that was less grotesque, I've become a much more thoughtful and considered person as a result. Anyone opinionated online hasn't lasted. Everyone gets dragged. Only the silent ones who we can project our ideas of perfection onto survive.'

It's great that we can hold people accountable – people hold me accountable all the time. Being held accountable when you mess up, say the wrong thing or handle a situation questionably *should* be a normal part of existing in online spaces, as long as that accountability is productive. But, equally, we don't want perpetrators dressing up abuse as holding someone 'accountable'. Abuse is abuse, whether that person made a mistake to trigger your reaction or not.

Doxxing is a tactic some use to attack trolls. On the surface, it might seem as if you're holding them accountable for their actions. But you're not – it's just punishment. We saw this during the Euros 2020, when racist tweets were posted after the England football team lost in the final. Greater Manchester Police were investigating the abusive social media accounts, but some people still took it upon themselves to discover who these trolls were – and found one of them who worked at Savills, one of the biggest real-estate companies. His photo and identity were revealed to the world and he was later fired from his job. But is this providing him an opportunity for growth? Is this the right intervention for behavioural change that we can all see? And we have to ask ourselves if all this tactic is really doing is teaching someone to be more subtle in their racism. If we find someone online, find out where they work and get them fired, what has that achieved in the fight against online abuse? What's stopping that person from going on to start a new, anonymous account where they can be even more vile and hateful than before?

It's like the death penalty, where all we're doing is killing people for killing people. It's a new form of that eye-for-an-eye mentality. There's a delicate line to tread. Taking matters into your own hands – if you choose to – should always be done carefully. You have to find a way to allow for constructive accountability, and not just be a reckless vigilante. It's not something I necessarily have an answer for, but we do need to be mindful of the urge to shame.

Allowing people to be better

When I spoke with Aja Barber – an author, stylist and consultant operating at the intersection between fashion and sustainability – she posed an interesting point: 'I'm held to account all the time. I get messages about things that I've not done well on my platform. And that's the only way you learn, right? Nobody is born knowing everything. You have to learn by someone being like, "Hey, you kind of did this wrong. Here's how you can do it better." And I get those messages, and the fact that people don't see that going down, doesn't mean that it doesn't happen. People feel because they don't actively see me getting criticized loads on my page, that it doesn't happen and there's no accountability for me.'

I think the difference between abuse and holding someone to account lies in the delivery. In Aja's case, any missteps are often handled behind the scenes, in a productive, educational way that's conducive to her doing better next time. That's accountability. But if someone makes a mistake online and it results in people dogpiling their profile, hurling vitriolic abuse at them about their identity, and them becoming fearful of remaining in the online space – that's abuse.

Accountability frameworks

The idea of demanding accountability is a pressing concern for those in the public domain. But how can we make sure it doesn't lead to online abuse if we haven't yet done the work when it comes to accountability frameworks online? We don't have robust mechanisms to hold public figures to account. So how do we call out a celebrity when they've done something wrong if it's not to @ them on Twitter or Instagram?

With racial tension at the forefront of sport, particularly football, they're taking a stand against racism, both offline and online. Many Premier League clubs are now banning racist fans from their grounds, sending a signal of solidarity and showing there should be no room for this kind of hate and that's not what the game is about. The next step I would like to see from clubs is creating appropriate forums for fans to have their concerns heard. Anger is never a justification for abuse, but anger does need an outlet. For example, when there were headlines in the international news about secret deals around a new European Super League, we saw fans had very little in the way of legitimate paths to be heard and have a say about their beloved club.

When it comes to MPs, there's an official channel to contact their office via email or letter, but there are no other means of holding them accountable. Mechanisms need to exist for people to be able to productively hold people in the public eye to account. Without the appropriate forums and channels to make complaints and provide feedback, and without widespread education on accountability, people's behaviour will continue to cross a boundary.

As it is, we're left in this growing cesspit on Twitter, trying to come up with accountability frameworks that inevitably spiral into hate. We need to hold tech companies and institutions to higher standards, pointing out the ways they're currently failing to support their users – and are making those in the public eye vulnerable to abuse because there's not an appropriate outlet for criticism.

So, what next?

Jameela Jamil is a prominent figure in online advocacy and change. But, in the absence of appropriate mechanisms and systems, she's had to take a different approach. 'The ways in which I am trying to hold big tech companies accountable is by constantly staying on their back. A foundation of social justice is being willing to be relentless and annoying. Disliked and misunderstood. And understanding that you'll make friends in social justice. But not that many. And because I know that, I've established myself as a tedious person for them to deal with. I lean into that.

'I'm happy and lucky that, somehow, my career has survived so many public beatings. I think it's important because a lot of women, in particular minorities, we cancel ourselves. People turn on us and we say, "I should probably leave now. I don't want to burden anyone any longer with my presence. I must go."

'I've always been the first one to call myself out. When everyone was praising me for being this great feminist, I was the first one to be like, "Hold on, no, I used to be a massive misogynist." And it's important people know that so they can see we all can carry internalized misogyny.'

As we've discovered, online abuse is a huge problem worldwide. And, as with offline harassment and abuse, it's complex. It's messy. Abusers won't just use one tactic; they'll use a combination. And they're all connected, with one impact leading to another in a terrible domino effect. To address this takes time and resources, and for all of us to play an active role in keeping online spaces safe, because even with the best intentions we could inflict harm on others.

So who are the key players in reversing this damage, and what can be done differently?

Chapter Four: Who are the key players in online abuse, and what can they do differently?

When it comes to innovation, we can see a pattern throughout history. Something new is created, it becomes popular, and we integrate it into our society and everyday lives before realizing there are unintended consequences and problems to solve. It takes enormous effort and often lengthy campaigns to crack down on the harmful issues created. If we're lucky, over time all the necessary changes will be implemented and we will have a regulatory framework and more appropriate behaviour.

Look at, for example, vehicles. The first automobile was built in 1885, and as cars started to become more prevalent, it wasn't uncommon to see people getting behind the wheel while under the influence of alcohol. So governments concluded that it should be illegal, leading to the introduction of drink-driving laws starting from 1910 in the US, and 1967 in the UK.

But even with these laws and increasing safety measures, it's still an ongoing fight we're trying to tackle as a society. Pubs and bars advertise taxi firms. Public safety campaigns around drink-driving have been around for over fifty years. Soaps – including my favourite, *EastEnders* – have storylines dedicated to raising awareness about its impacts. All of us playing our part to keep our roads safe is now ingrained in our culture, whether that's organizing a ride home ahead of time on a night out, or speaking up when someone even contemplates drink-driving. And this is how it works for plenty of other industries and technologies. Tobacco, the use of coal and oil – it took time for us to realize how we should approach them as a society, and how we can make changes for the better.

So when we scratch our heads and wonder what we can do about online abuse, the playbook is right in front of us. We do what we've done before: we regulate and demand appropriate health and safety standards. We invest in public education, we empower, we incentivize and, where necessary, we force influential players and institutions to play their part.

In short, we all need to come together to stand up against online abuse.

This is easier said than done when online abuse is still a new concept to many of us. When you're in the thick of an issue, it can be hard to see what the problems are and where they're rooted. So what – or perhaps more accurately, **who** – is perpetuating the problem?

The key players

There are key players who knowingly and unknowingly prop up online abuse – from the highest authorities and tech leaders all the way down to people in our own communities. Knowing the 'who' behind the problem is as important as knowing what the problem is. As part of our digital self-care toolkit, we have to understand the risks around us and how they feed into the issue. Once we do that, then we can look at what can be changed. After all, scientists don't jump straight to solutions or recommendations; they first examine different causes and behaviours to find out why something happens. And yes, this might include some self-examination – how do we as individuals contribute to the problem? Actions to prevent drink-driving came from everyone understanding that our roads weren't safe and that it was everyone's responsibility to make sure they were.

Online abuse is a worldwide problem that needs both local and global solutions, yet there's been little to no intervention by governments at any level – and where there has, it's been slow. In terms of my own campaign to effect change, it's taken over five years to convince those in power that online violence is even a real issue that needs addressing. Now I'm finally being invited to UN panels, tech councils, government committee meetings and conferences to talk about what government and tech companies can do. We need people with the power to make changes to see that there's something chronically wrong with the status quo.

Through countless talks and presentations that I've held, I've seen the same argument again and again: 'There are no solutions to ending online abuse.' But the reality is that there are no **simple** solutions.

We shouldn't have to keep fighting multiple fights when it comes to online abuse. Battling the police, trying to get our abuse taken seriously. Struggling to get through to tech companies and stop them making it so easy for violent people to thrive. Spending years campaigning to change policies, despite tech changing almost daily. Resisting our own feelings to save face around friends, family and loved ones. Ignoring the isolation we feel because we can't talk about our abuse – and the alienation, victim blaming or lack of understanding from the other party when we do. Not to mention pushing governments and social media companies to provide resources and support to those who need it, including the civil society organizations around the world who are raising awareness of the threats to our online spaces on a shoestring budget. Our online safety must be properly resourced, with training and capacity building for women and other historically underrepresented groups.

It's relentless.

At the same time, we all have a part to play. We can't only look in one direction and point fingers. We can't rest on our laurels and say, 'Well, when the government fixes the policies, then real change will happen.' When you take this approach to making a difference, nothing happens. Tech giants look to the government, the government looks to education, education looks to the general public. Meanwhile, our online spaces continue to be hijacked and weaponized. We can **all** contribute to changing the nature and reducing the scale and effect of online abuse in digital spaces.

It's not enough to simply say that there are bad people in the world, so of course there are bad people in online spaces. As a society we need to replicate what we did around drink-driving. Change policies. Introduce rules and regulations. Create standards for being a digital citizen. Write storylines about the issue in soaps. Tighten up on algorithms to prevent them from amplifying harm.

But to challenge the status quo and start effecting the change we need, we must first delve deeper into who holds the power. Let's begin with the ones hosting it all: the tech companies.

Tech companies

Although we all have a shared responsibility to make online spaces safe for everyone, tech companies like Meta (Facebook's parent organization), Twitter, Twitch, Google, Apple, Snapchat and Reddit hold the greatest share. Start-ups and even special-interest forums too! It reminds me of what renowned computer scientist and inventor of the World Wide Web Tim Berners-Lee once said: 'For people who want to make sure the Web serves humanity, we have to concern ourselves with what people are building on top of it.'

And tech companies have certainly built something. All of the social media platforms are great for connecting and reaching the masses. I said as much earlier in the book; social media was a tool to reach other young people when I was running for the Youth Council election. Social media is full of potential – but that's the problem. It's full of potential for **everyone**, whether they want to connect with other fans of a TV show or sling slurs at women in the public eye. If you've never experienced online abuse before, it can be difficult to imagine just how overwhelming simply opening one of the apps can be. You don't know if the first thing you'll see is something kind or disgustingly offensive. And what can you do about it? Barely anything at all. Should you even have to do something? In an ideal world, no. That task should be on the shoulders of the tech companies. But it definitely seems as if the tech bros in charge can't – or simply **won't** – bring about that change.

'Tech bros' isn't some cool indie-band name. The term labels the disproportionate numbers of white, middle-class males in places like Silicon Valley who are creating fast-moving, innovative and world-changing technologies without nearly enough consideration of women, people of colour, and the disabled and LGBTQIA+ communities. A lot of this has to do with the lack of diversity and inclusivity behind the scenes. Most of the tech giants were built by this Silicon Valley tech-bro crowd.

Of course, this is nothing new. We live in a patriarchal world, and those of us who aren't cis and white are used to adapting to things that aren't created with us in mind. But the sooner we accept this as fact online as well, the sooner we can put in place the necessary boundaries to make ourselves safer online, as well as encouraging existing – and upcoming – platforms to evolve alongside their users, not against them.

The silence from social media companies when reporting abuse is a chronic issue. And that's not good enough. In July 2020, rapper Talib Kweli was suspended from Twitter after incessantly tweeting at and about Black women, in particular twenty-four-year-old student Maya Moody. He did this for twelve hours straight in a single day. During that intense period, Black women around the world participated in a campaign to report Kweli for targeted harassment and get him suspended. It took almost two weeks for something to happen. Two weeks of women having to shout about it before Twitter did something.

When we talk about new tech and policy-making, women are

constantly being left behind. This results in social media platforms, algorithms and tech reproducing and exacerbating the same inequalities, the same harms and the same biases found offline.

A conversation I had with Alix Dunn – tech expert and founder of the Engine Room, an international organization that helps activists and other social change agents to make the most of data and technology and increase their impact – gave me a fresh perspective. She explained that you have to be incredibly arrogant to think you can build something that's appropriate for everyone. That you can conduct user research on your own and create something that caters to all intersections. And not only building and designing it alone, but also governing it as you scale. That you can grow and roll out to new countries and new cultures without any user backlash or adversity. It's unrealistic.

Tech companies may not have invented the patriarchy, nor white supremacy, but they are responsible for the scale and spread of its online effects (and damage) at life-threatening speeds. These companies need to make a significant commitment to diversity and inclusion – internally **and** externally. This should include a serious investment in working with academics and civil society groups in order to implement culturally sensitive policies and algorithms. Doing this would be a huge step towards building trust and proving to us as users that they aren't putting profits over people.

Ultimately, tech companies have a responsibility to make our online space a much less scary place to be part of, and that starts with putting accountability frameworks in place that require tech companies to hold bad actors (including abusive users) accountable. And also frameworks that hold tech companies themselves accountable.

I asked Azmina Dhrodia for her thoughts, and she felt that platforms need to make it very clear that abuse and violence against women and other minoritized genders are absolutely not tolerated in these spaces. In cases where it does occur – because, sadly, it probably always will – there needs to be a system in place where women feel they are heard and can get justice. At the moment, this isn't always or consistently happening, and too much damage to the relationship between women and online social platforms has been done.

So how can tech companies begin to build that trust and make their platforms safe for all?

Representation internally and externally

Following George Floyd's murder in May 2020, eventual attempts have been made by most tech companies to diversify their workforce, but there's been little progress on reimagining and redesigning these spaces or the business models of tech companies. Tech companies need to do more to address gender-based and intersectional abuse on their platforms, in particular abuse targeting Black and minoritized women. But we've seen countless times how they don't do that. I'm tired of being the conduit between grass-roots organizations and companies like Twitter, Facebook and Instagram. Not because I don't want to help my friends, but because the platforms should have better systems in place.

Without diverse talent working within these companies or inclusive engagement, minoritized voices won't be heard. They need to take an intersectional approach – and not just to tick corporate social responsibility (CSR) diversity boxes, but because they acknowledge the immense value gained by bringing different viewpoints to the table. Here's an example of the hoops civil society groups have to jump through online. On the eve of Menstrual Hygiene Day 2020, a number of period-equity charities were shadowbanned on Instagram. Shadowbanning is the act of banning someone on a platform without them knowing. Their posts and comments are hidden from their audience, with no way to push their message to the masses. The fact this is done in a cloak-and-dagger kind of way makes the matter worse. 'Shadowbanning', unsurprisingly, isn't an official Instagram term. But it's the digital equivalent of being minimized and silenced. Except, more often than not, it never seems to happen to perpetrators of abuse and those causing genuine harm. Only to those who need to make their voices heard – especially if they're coming from an intersectional perspective and trying to make a positive difference.

In this instance, it was only because Gabby Jahanshahi-Edlin, founder of BGP and a personal friend, noticed this was happening and we talked about it amongst our collective community that we knew they were shadowbanned, otherwise it would have been hard to spot. There was nothing transparent or clear around what happened to their accounts, and the platforms denied the ban altogether. With my access to the right people at Meta, we were able to do something. But this still forced Gabby and the BGP team to embark on a journey of emotional labour – having to repeatedly explain the situation. Every time I escalate a case to a social media platform, I always sign off by saying that I shouldn't need to write this email, and nor am I the only one who signs off in this way. Tech companies need transparent community engagement processes. We shouldn't have to rely on small organizations operating on a minuscule budget to pick up Meta's slack.

When perpetrators break the law by attacking someone online because of their race, there aren't clear repercussions. There also doesn't seem to be much of an incentive for tech companies to change their platforms in ways that would provide vulnerable users with greater freedom and safety.

All the current improvements we have in tech are coming from marginalized communities, like those who spoke up about Menstrual Hygiene Day and, hours later, were able to post as normal again. In May 2020, whistle-blower Ifeoma Ozoma came forward with allegations of discrimination and racism at Pinterest. Eighteen months later, Ifeoma is a key figure in helping other tech employees disclose and fight against mistreatment at work – she was even instrumental in changing the law in California! And this is great. But it's also time for the wealthiest of the wealthy to understand what online abuse is and to do something meaningful about it.

This is not to say that companies have made no attempts to tackle the issue – as mentioned earlier, there have been moves to diversify the tech workforce. But Hera Hussain has pointed out how this doesn't solve the problem: 'When platforms have been made aware of diversity issues in their teams, they have made lots of great strides in hiring more diverse teams. But the people they tend to hire are based in the United States. Yes, they might be people of colour, but they absolutely cannot claim to understand the living reality of people in Zambia or the rest of the world. The way we define diversity has become how close you are to whiteness. And they are very close to whiteness because they grew up in that society. They're not going to understand the cultural nuances that people face every day in the Global South.'

That attitude bleeds into their entire operation. It's difficult for companies to judge what is or isn't appropriate if they don't have the full picture. Making a difference is about more than a few token hires. It's not enough to have one person from a diverse community. One Black woman on a tech company safety board is not going to speak to the experiences of all Black women on a global scale. So, in addition to hiring a diverse workforce at all levels, tech companies need to adopt an inclusive, well-resourced and diverse engagement practice with civil society and academia around the world.

When we have more people who can speak expertly on various topics, from a huge range of perspectives and diverse identities, and tech companies are open to hearing these conversations and facilitating them themselves, we will begin to see a real shift in representation.

Transparency

It's time for tech companies to provide greater transparency about their content moderation efforts. This includes allowing trusted research institutions and civil society organizations to access anonymized and disaggregated data about content removals and complaints submitted to the platforms. What should this include? At the very least, it would be helpful to have insights into the type of action taken, the time it takes to review reported content, and increased transparency around the appeal process.

The COVID-19 pandemic showed how muddy the waters are when it comes to the boundaries tech companies set and how they choose to enforce them. During this time, the nature of public health and safety – and measures such as wearing masks and keeping our distance from one another – became heavily politicized. Even heads of state, like Donald Trump, weighed in and added their own falsehoods. Tech companies took steps to limit pandemic-related misinformation on their platforms. They added content warnings that explicitly called the source into question. Twitter eventually banned Donald Trump in relation to his tweets about the violent United States Capitol attack on 6 January 2021. It was (eventually) the right move.

But it made many question why this hadn't been done for other harmful content that had existed for many years before COVID-19 misinformation. If it was easy enough to take these steps to stop the spread of misinformation about the pandemic, why couldn't they do so for racism? Or gendered disinformation? Or homophobia? Or any conspiracy that threatens the dignity and human rights of minoritized communities?

This comes back to transparency. We don't know why tech platforms drew the line where they did. As it is, we're in the dark. In Glitch's *Ripple Effect* report, we heard from many women and non-binary people who were frustrated by the inconsistency:

> 'They aren't doing enough to address online abuse.'
> 'Offensive posts are never taken down.'
> 'Responses from social media companies are often non-existent.'

A culturally sensitive and people-centric approach

As users of online platforms, we need insight into policies related to dehumanizing language based on gender, ethnicity and other protected categories. Policies should be regularly reviewed and updated to address new trends, patterns and manifestations of online abuse, including violence against women and people with intersecting identities.

While we're at it, tech companies also need to provide more financial support to civil society organizations working with marginalized communities to tackle this abuse and harassment, and fund digital-citizenship education initiatives. They should look to cooperate with anti-racist, LGBTQIA+ and women's advocacy organizations to fund research into the impact of gender-based and intersectional online abuse, and how gender identity and expression, sexual orientation and ethnicity play a role in online abuse.

Talking to Asha Allen about it, she said: 'There's a lack of nuanced understanding when it comes to online violence and online abuse. I think we've seen it in the conversations happening with the Euros. Some of the stuff I've been seeing is in regards to "How does a monkey emoji equate to racism?" And there's a very obvious answer to this. But it's where context and nuance are so necessary.

'We don't want automated content moderation; that's not going to pick up or allow people to help the development of a contextual understanding at this moment in time. I can't go on Twitter and provide them with contextual understanding or analysis of how this particular post is violent or abusive. I have to go through these clickbox exercises which, sure, they've gotten more comprehensive over time. But what if I want to opt in to giving you more data to be able to help your systems improve?'

How can AI ever understand the nuance? And then, beyond that, how can you ensure a human being understands it?

Content moderation needs to be improved. I worked with one tech company to help it understand how it could handle the N-word. Yes, you could say 'ban it', but there are some people in the Black community who use the N-word comfortably. Or take the word 'queer'. To some, it's a slur. To some members of the LGBTQIA+ community, it can be a term that's been reclaimed. These nuanced conversations are necessary, but are not being had on a wide or regular enough scale.

Tech companies need to ensure that members of both their policy and their content moderation teams are coming from a range of lived experiences and identities, to ensure that they can have these policy and process discussions in a nuanced way. This will allow holistic and inclusive risk assessments to identify potential pitfalls. It may also require investing a proportion of their multibillion-dollar profits to hire consultants who are able to provide those diverse perspectives and guide such conversations independently.

Reporting

There's a real need to be clear about what happens in the reporting process on these platforms. When you write a letter of complaint, there's a known process: the letter is put in the post box or dropped off at the post office; it then gets sent to a distribution centre where it is sorted and sent out for delivery. You know what its destination is and our right to a written response. But when we report harmful content online, where does it go and what decisions are made?

Reporting processes need to be improved and made easier for users. Those affected shouldn't have to jump through multiple hoops to get even a small sense of justice. As it stands, responses to complaints aren't timely enough, if they come at all. And the highly abusive content being reported can remain on the platform for hours – sometimes days – after the initial complaint.

Not only that, more needs to be done to identify repeat offenders and make it difficult for those with accounts that have been banned from platforms to resurface. IP addresses linked to permanently deleted accounts should not be able to create new accounts for a significant period of time. Despite attempts to implement IP bans for repeat offenders, there are still ways for perpetrators to jump right back on and pick up where they left off, easily circumnavigating their ban (some use VPNs, virtual private networks, for example). And there's nothing to deter them from doing it again and again – no concrete punishment.

There's a tendency for tech companies to take a hands-off approach to abuse, instead leaving it for the affected parties to sort out amongst themselves. But that isn't something that should be put on the shoulders of the minoritized. Nor are the perpetrators usually the kind to engage in good-faith debate.

If tech companies would deal with these issues themselves on the front-end, it would eliminate hours of wasted time on behind-the-scenes conversations. No more tiresome back-and-forth between victims, the police and tech platforms. Just them taking the initiative and banning people when needed.

Duty of care

In 2019, a proposal for a duty-of-care standard for tech companies was developed by William Perrin and Lorna Woods. Both are experts on the issues of regulation and free speech, and their calls for change were backed up by years of experience. William has worked on technology policy since the 1990s, and was a driving force behind the creation of Ofcom, the government-approved body overlooking broadcasting and telecommunication standards in the UK. During his time advising the Cabinet Office, he worked closely on regulatory regimes in many economic and social sectors. Lorna is a professor of internet law at the University of Essex. She is an EU national expert on free speech and data regulation, and was formerly a solicitor in private practice specializing in telecommunications, media and technology law.

'Duty of care' is a helpful piece of terminology when discussing the health and safety standards we should expect from tech companies. Put simply, it's the notion that they have a duty to protect their users, and a failure to do so should have legal consequences for that company. This doesn't mean tech companies have to be perfect, just that they must do all they can to provide sufficient care. As it is, tech companies aren't really held to account for their role in the situation. A push for duty of care would make them active participants, meaning they would have to start taking charge.

One issue is that there's no real financial incentive for tech companies to take responsibility, but we need to start building platforms that make money in more ethical ways. I once spoke on a panel at the House of Lords with Kenny Ethan Jones – a model, writer, advocate, consultant and proud trans man – who raised an interesting point on the motivations of tech companies: 'It depends on how the platforms make money. It depends on their system. Platforms such as Instagram want to foster hate because you spend more time on the platform, so it is not in their best interest to do the right thing. Reversing the algorithms so we can see posts in chronological order rather than prioritizing content that will keep us engaged (and outraged) is just one of many practical changes they can make. But, if it is not in their interest, the bigger platforms won't be regulating themselves.'

One of Kenny's points seemed scarily prescient when Facebook whistle-blower Frances Haugen came forward in 2021 about the company's unwillingness to sacrifice profit. She claimed Facebook was 'making hate worse' and that senior executives weren't interested in fixing the problem. In Haugen's words, Facebook didn't want 'to accept even little slivers of profit being sacrificed for safety'.

The business models of platforms like Facebook are closely linked to the 'attention economy'. The Center for Humane Technology explains this as: 'The seemingly free social media products we use every day help us to stay connected, learn new things, and find information. But they also analyze our actions and the data we share, using what they learn about us to trick us into paying attention to them more than we want. They sell that attention – and ultimately changes in what we think and how we behave – to advertisers. These social media products are caught in a race to capture our attention in order to make money.'

The commodification of attention could have multiple positive benefits for the individual and wider society. However, going by Frances Haugen's statements, in practice it's not about altruistic motives. Rage, anger and polarization are fuelling further hate, keeping people engaged and participating in these online ecosystems.

Content about Idris Elba, Adele or cute babies is what keeps me engaged on platforms. Live-tweeting while watching an awards show or the latest episode of *Euphoria* (when it's already two hours past my bedtime) is a joy that keeps my attention. The one that platforms encourage. But a barrage of abuse? That's not going to get me to want to pay more attention to that platform.

On YouTube, if you want your channel to grow, it needs engagement, and this includes comments. Even negative ones. So a video that sets out to be hated and receive thousands of negative comments is going to do 'quite well'. But people shouldn't want that. That isn't healthy growth. It should be part of tech companies' duty of care that they promote engagement that brings people together, not interactions that tear them apart.

Investing in safety tools

In 2021, Frances Haugen's statements and a series of reports in the *Wall Street Journal* revealed something many campaigners and organizations in the digital rights and gender space have known for a long time. Something millions of survivors know too. That companies such as Facebook can do so much more to address hate on their platforms, but make an active choice to put profits over people.

What was disappointing was how much Facebook had made bystander reporting more difficult. This is a hugely important tool and intervention that not only supports victims of online abuse but also helps clean up the internet and remove harmful content. Unsurprising, but still damaging.

Companies should be providing users with the safety tools they need to protect themselves and others. It should be one of their highest priorities. Users should have access to greater controls and filters in their online experiences, to ensure that they have agency and decision-making power when it comes to the type of content they see on social media and which users can or can't communicate with them. It sounds like a lot, but it isn't. It really isn't.

What next?

On the surface, these all seem like large-scale changes, but they don't have to be. Many of these recommendations are simple to implement and we could begin to see the shift now – if tech companies were willing to take those steps. A for-profit company like Meta has the resources and experts to do this. Their quarterly revenue (at the time of writing) is expected to be $31.5 billion. They have the weight behind them to make a statement of intent and allocate some of their profits to the kinds of recommendations I've made. User safety is an expectation of every industry, and tech shouldn't be any different.

It's time to change the direction we're heading in; at the very least to put a stop to moving fast and breaking things – breaking people – and to multibillion-dollar tech companies monopolizing the tech market. At the time of writing, Elon Musk, founder of Tesla, is reported to have made an offer of $44 billion to own Twitter, with an alarming pledge to refocus free speech: 'free speech' here meaning let's be more relaxed about online abuse. It's time for tech companies to acknowledge the part they play in online toxicity, and to put their foot down firmly and (a dream here) give users greater power as consumers. This is a klaxon for government both to incentivize and to force tech operations to improve.

It's time to be better.

Government

Since the early 2000s, tech companies have pretty much been responsible for their own regulation. So it might seem as if it's solely up to them to make changes and lead by example. But there's another player that should be involved: our governments. They also have a duty of care to their citizens, and should be doing everything they can to keep them safe. I touched on this earlier – when cars were invented, they eventually brought in laws to regulate how they were used. Speed limits, mandatory seat belts, no drinking and driving. All changes made with the express purpose of keeping people safe.

Social media is just another in a long line of innovations that need government oversight to keep them in check. As we've seen, when tech companies are left to their own devices, profit often comes before people. They need governments to step in and ensure they're on the right track to putting people first. This means legislation and regulation. Without it, it's likely little will happen.

Right now, we don't have what we need. And the online abuse we see happening to minoritized groups can't be effectively minimized until there is government intervention.

We know that abuse is abuse. But some types of abuse are not acknowledged within a legal framework, and victims find that the acts committed against them are swept under the rug. Racist violence online is unacceptable, but gender-based violence online is glazed over. We saw it with my story – I had to fight for justice for some of my abuse and ignore the rest of it, based on the lack of legislation. Since online gender-based violence isn't a recognized offence, even though women are more vulnerable to attacks.

This is the unfortunate state of legislation right now. You would think something would have happened sooner given how women politicians are disproportionately abused compared to their male counterparts. But it again comes back to the patriarchy. Progress moves slowly because the people in charge just don't see it on the scale that their minoritized and women colleagues do.

Governments should be ensuring that any response to gender-based violence online also includes an intersectional analysis and addresses the particular risks faced by women and girls from marginalized and racialized communities. This includes both data collection and publishing gender-disaggregated statistics about the prevalence and types of – and response to – online abuse faced by these communities in particular.

So where are we currently? That depends on where you are in the world. In the UK, an Online Safety Bill has just been redrafted. In the European Union, the Digital Services Act is pushing forward. Both have the same purpose: to create a safer, fairer internet. When we consider the global legislative landscape around online abuse, it's important to consider the good or promising practices as well as bad practices. That's how we can come together to create stronger legislation. The Online Safety Bill and Digital Services Act are both being developed at the same time. There's an opportunity there for the UK government and the EU to learn from one another, without using this as a power-grabbing opportunity.

We need this approach to legislation, but on a global scale. Several countries have abandoned a gender-neutral stance, acknowledging that women are more affected by online abuse. By doing this, and accepting that online abuse is part of the continuum of violence against women, they can work towards mitigating, minimizing and ending it. And when we do that, women can go back to finding joy in being part of an online community, free to express themselves.

The Office of the eSafety Commissioner in Australia is the world's first government agency committed to keeping its citizens safer online, and has a programme – Women In The Spotlight (WITS) – to elevate and protect women's voices online. It is also becoming increasingly intersectional in its approach, recognizing other at-risk online groups and setting out to protect them as well. These include Aboriginal and Torres Strait Islander peoples, culturally and linguistically diverse people, people living with disabilities, the LGBTQIA+ community, and the young and old.

In the UK, there are existing frameworks and conventions that could be utilized to strengthen this policy area. For example, the Domestic Abuse Act was passed in April 2021 as a means to create a statutory definition of domestic abuse. But there's a further step that could be taken: ratifying the Istanbul Convention. This would be a commitment to preventing violence against women, not just responding to it. Or incorporating the Convention on the Elimination of All Forms of Discrimination against Women into domestic law. While the UK government has agreed to both of these important frameworks, the lack of implementation to date has meant that a lack of progress has been made in terms of ending violence against women – which would ensure all users are protected online.

And that's also part of the problem. We need to improve the political process. Making new laws is slow and laborious. It can take years of campaigning before change is considered. But technology evolves at a monumental pace. The game can shift overnight. The speed of our actions needs to catch up with it.

But, aside from changing the foundations of their process, what more should our governments be doing?

Regulation

In my interview with Jac sm Kee, she brought up the point that with so much money tied up in their platforms, why would tech companies ever change? 'Unless they fundamentally change their bottom line – which they will never do because they're a business – social media is not the space to address such a systemic complex.'

That's why we need government intervention and regulation. It's an opportunity to spark positive competition between tech companies, and force them to do better and invest in safety tools. Right now, it's a race to the bottom. The focus is on creating platforms that people flock to, with standard policies that result in minimal protection for users and a laxity when it comes to privacy settings. They make billions from our data, likes and interactions. Yet we have no oversight – on either a personal or a government level. We need something that's far better than what we currently have, with a handful of companies controlling all the tech. It's something we see every time Facebook goes down; it isn't just Facebook – it's Instagram and WhatsApp too. US politician Alexandria Ocasio-Cortez has been particularly critical of the state of the industry, calling it 'monopolistic behaviour' and criticizing Facebook's blasé attitude in the face of people who depend on their platforms to communicate.

It has to go further than that though. Regulation has to focus on women and intersectional identities. Unfortunately, the Online Safety Bill proposed in 2022 didn't mention violence against women or gender once. Despite a BBC *Panorama* investigation finding that trolls were being pushed towards misogynistic hate through recommendations and links suggested by algorithms on five of the most popular social media sites. They found that profiles were being sent into a spiral of hate and conspiracies. You can't talk about online safety without also talking about the abuse women receive. Regulations that don't take into account violence against women are failing to make the online space safe for everyone.

There's no one simple fix that covers every demographic. No easy solution that covers everything. And it's not a one-and-done issue, either. It's something that needs revisiting every time something new comes along and is balanced with our other freedoms. Tech moves fast, and the government needs to keep up with it. In the UK, our most recent legislative change was the Communications Act 2003. Before that, it was the Malicious Communications Act 1988, dealing with letters and articles. Policy changes that we need as a necessity haven't been reviewed properly in decades, and in that time we've seen the launch of Facebook, Instagram, Snapchat, AI algorithms, deep and machine learning, facial recognition and the metaverse.

And this is only looking at one country. The UK's legislation and governmental representation – even with its flaws – are leagues ahead of some others. Many countries are yet to see women as anything other than second-class citizens – let alone recognizing that different identities can intersect and make individuals especially vulnerable online. It's time to bring legislation in line with the world that we live in, and avoid a split-net where tech companies and users adhere to very different laws.

A public health approach

Similar to the drink-driving campaigns, it takes support across the board to effect positive change. We need to see a comprehensive public health approach towards online abuse. If governments aren't going to introduce new legislation any time soon, they *can* push campaigns that outline clear recommendations for employers and teachers so they can encourage their employees and students to stay safe online. There should be public guidance on what digital safety means. What we all need in relation to online safety is a suite of training, skills and resources. Governments should be providing a road map for digital health and safety.

For many industries, this conversation tends to focus on the physicality of health and safety. Even when it comes to mental health, it's from a physical point of view – how does being in the office affect someone? How does mental stress affect someone's physical well-being? The conversation rarely recognizes that someone's health and safety can be compromised by experiences on the World Wide Web.

If digital health-and-safety training could be undertaken by law enforcement and front-line workers too, then even better. With government support, we could have sensitivity training that teaches law enforcement what is and isn't acceptable when they meet those affected by online abuse. To be aware of the intersectional issues at play. To treat victims with care and respect. I've experienced how difficult dealing with the police can be first-hand. And my story isn't the only one. In Glitch's *Ripple Effect* report, this is what someone else had to say about their experience: 'I reported the online harassment to local law enforcement, as there were physical threats via Facebook and Instagram from a stranger. There was no follow-through from the police.'

There isn't enough focus on the legislation around online abuse and best-practice policies for supporting victims. The government needs to implement specific training that shows law enforcement the scope of online hate crimes, highlights recent changes to Crown Prosecution Service guidelines, and emphasizes how seriously such cases should be treated. Any training should be developed in consultation with civil society organizations (small and large) and experts in this area.

For the victims, the government should also provide support services such as helplines, as well as refuges for those experiencing online abuse in the context of intimate partner violence. And annual reports on online abuse would arm small organizations like Glitch with the information we need to better support people.

But it goes beyond helping victims. Part of a public health approach should be addressing the drivers of online violence in the first place.

We need to look at who is committing these acts and figure out how we can reach them before hate does. Or consider how we can rehabilitate them and their abusive mindset, bringing them out of that cycle.

Some level of government support would go a long way in making even incremental changes. That's why having the right voices in the right places is needed before making any legislative adjustments. Those can come in time. In the here and now, marginalized voices in positions of power can speak up and drive attitude shifts, if only governments would let them.

Digital citizenship education

We have a lot of work to do when it comes to dealing with and addressing the growing apathy of people online. There's a lot of social good that's been achieved, but there's still a way to go. In the UK, the government's Digital Services Tax, which came into effect on 1 April 2020, imposes a 2 per cent tax on tech giants such as Meta, Google and Twitter. Why not ring-fence at least 10 per cent of this new revenue annually to fund efforts to address online abuse more effectively? Or use it to invest in digital citizenship education and resources?

We can point fingers at the government but the reality is that we play a part too. Good citizens have rights, but we also have responsibilities. We have a right to education, but it's our responsibility to work hard at school. We have a right to the NHS, but we have a responsibility to not take advantage. We receive this basic education and understanding of citizenship and what it means to be a citizen of our country. Yet we don't have any of that when it comes to the online space.

Above and beyond policy changes, there are ways the government can effect positive movement through employment, education and beyond.

We're well into the twenty-first century, yet we don't have a curriculum educating young people about being good digital citizens. There are fantastic opportunities for entering the tech sphere, such as courses on coding and scholarships to encourage young women to get into STEM fields. But there aren't any guidelines on how to innovate that space responsibly.

When we're little, we learn the golden rules. Treat others as we wish to be treated. At sixteen, we receive basic sex education to teach us how not to get pregnant and how to protect ourself against STIs. We can get our driver's licence at age seventeen, and there's the whole Highway Code to read and study to keep us and others around us safe.

But where are the golden rules for social media? Who's providing the road map to navigate the tech world safely? We need an ethical framework around algorithms to help us understand the online space, and online abuse, better. A framework that helps us make better decisions, protects us from harm, and teaches us how to handle abuse if it does happen.

The government should instil digital citizenship education from an early age, and teach children to create ethical, healthy relationships with tech – as well as creating platforms for social good and something other than pure profit at the expense of minoritized communities. By doing this, we will eliminate many of the problems we see in the digital world today.

For me, I was starting high school when the internet was just beginning to grow. In the UK, that's when you're eleven, and it was the time when MSN was taking off. That was pretty much all we had. Fast-forward to where it's now an everyday, essential part of life. You have a generation of teenagers discovering their bodies and hormones, but now with the added pressure of the internet. Toxicity can spill over into video games, social media platforms, group chats and the metaverse. Not to mention the ease with which content is accessed. It's effortless for teens to share graphic and inappropriate content. And if they're growing up feeling like this is the norm, they take these habits into adulthood and perpetuate a vicious cycle.

What we need is better education. The government should make this a mandatory part of the curriculum. Young people need to learn how to be active allies, why digital self-care is critical, how to be safe online, but also how to be brave online. Despite what trolls say, online safety isn't about censorship and stifling freedom of speech. It's knowing where to draw the line, how to treat people like the human beings they are, and how to stay safe. Digital citizenship education would give everyone the ability to use online technology confidently, respectfully and positively. It would prepare all users to navigate the constantly changing digital space and enable them to build more positive online communities.

So let's start encouraging these conversations with after-school clubs led by skilled specialists, or even in our libraries. When you equip children, you can equip their parents too – and it becomes a larger support network.

But it's not just about education at school level. It's about educating people of all ages. It's up to our governments to ensure that citizens are equipped with a general understanding of ethics and laws related to digital spaces, and that they know how to access advice, justice and redress on issues related to online safety.

Governments should also provide guidance to employers on the measures they must take to ensure employees are protected from online harassment, in both remote and office workplace environments. Although any measures to protect employees from online harms remain at the discretion of companies, national guidance on best practices is urgently needed.

The government also has a key responsibility to make sure that tech companies prioritize digital citizenship on their platforms. They can do this by outlining clear roles and responsibilities for technology companies, organizations and workplaces to promote good digital citizenship through policy and practices.

By providing digital safety and self-care resources as part of a public health approach to ending online abuse, governments can help ensure that all digital citizens are able to safely, freely, equally and competently navigate and use online spaces.

Improving access to justice and investing in research

I believe a lot of people have a false sense of security when it comes to online safety. There's this inherent belief that the government, the police and the law will have our backs online because there is legislation in place for similar abuse offline. But it doesn't work that way. If someone makes their intent to rape offline clear, that's at least recognized as assault, and there are steps to access justice. However, if a similar threat is made online, or there are threats made about what a person would do to the victim's body, no crime has technically been committed unless the act is completed. Say consensual pictures are taken and threatened to be shared without permission. Until they're distributed, the offence hasn't happened. Unless that person then commits a different crime, such as blackmail, the police can deem the situation to be low-risk, and it has the potential to be overlooked and minimized.

This is part of the problem, and somewhere the government could step in. In the long term this means making the necessary legislative changes, but something that would help in the meantime is making sure the avenues to justice are clear. Ensure people know how they can find support. That they feel safe in reporting any crime. Like with my story, it's painful to have to revisit these traumatic moments, especially when it doesn't feel like there's empathy.

Tying into the issue of representation, we need people in these supportive positions who know what we're going through. And knowing the right steps to take to make people feel comfortable means researching what women and minoritized communities experience.

But that's also an issue. There's very little research into the impact of online abuse on women and Black and minoritized communities, and intersectional online abuse. Quality studies could teach us so much. And what if they did so while working closely with women's organizations? They could provide the insights into gender-based and intersectional online abuse that authorities need, allowing them to make more informed decisions on the matter.

Mental health support

Without the right support, trauma from online abuse – no matter how small – can have lasting impacts on you, greatly affecting the quality of your life.

Because we're only just beginning to have these conversations in the way we should be, mental health support is severely lacking. Even if you're fortunate enough to have a therapist with the right expertise, people intending to support you can end up minimizing your abuse or exacerbating the damage without even realizing it.

It took me two rounds of therapy to get my diagnosis of PTSD. I spent eight weeks on a waiting list here in the UK; others don't even have that. You'll then spend half of your first session trying to explain what happened. Then, when you've rehashed your trauma, the response is, 'Well, could you block them?' The support for online abuse is unbelievably behind the times.

When I spoke with Laura Bates of the Everyday Sexism Project, she was open about her experience: 'We were talking about some specific things about having gone into schools and then having boys attempt to kind of online-stalk you afterwards and doxx you. If you explain it to anyone else, they kind of glaze over or they don't get it. And even in mainstream spaces where I had hoped that I might be able to find support through counselling and therapy, the effort of trying to explain this whole world that you're in, how it operates and how it works, to somebody who has no reference point into that world and no experience of it, becomes exhausting. Before you can get any support, everything requires an hour's explanation. and before you know it, it's the end of your session.'

Better, more appropriate, mental health services start with the government. They can fund programmes that help people heal in the ways they need to. For example, they could use a portion of the Digital Services Tax to invest in bespoke mental health support services. What we're dealing with is trauma, and that means specific trauma-trained professionals are needed. It's a specialist area of treatment, and done in the wrong way it can have adverse effects. Government money should go to trauma-focused CBT and eye movement desensitization and reprocessing (EMDR) therapy, with clear signposting that this is something you can request.

What next?

Hurt people hurt. If left unchecked, minimized and unacknowledged, trauma will eventually create more unconscious – or even conscious – perpetrators, and the circle will never end.

So let's become better digital citizens. Let's recognize that the trauma of online abuse is real and not some minor annoyance that blocking will solve. And let's encourage this same understanding across education, law enforcement, the government and mental health spaces too.

The media

The media can use its influence to sway public discourse, and so has the power to be a positive force when it comes to online abuse. But, as it is right now, it can sometimes feel like another roadblock in the

way of justice and change. One that's more obsessed with big headlines than pushing society forward.

It's a double-edged sword. On one hand, it's an incredible platform
to get your word out there. When ITV London asked me to do an
interview after my viral video incident, I saw it as an opportunity to
provoke change. To be a powerful Black woman telling my experiences
with online abuse. However, I also had to play the game and not be the
'angry Black woman'. Nor the sad and fragile woman. And this was just
twenty-four hours after being told that somebody wanted to cut my
clitoris off.

I had to take on that responsibility because you can't trust the
media to put forward the best perception of you off their own backs.
You have to navigate how you will be portrayed, because their priority is not your well-being or the aftermath. It's how many eyeballs
they can get watching or reading. The vigilance is exhausting.

Every thirty seconds, a woman is abused on Twitter. That means
in the time it's taking you to read this book, thousands of women
are going through this experience. Most of these women don't have
the privilege of their story being picked up by journalists. They can't
just walk into a news station and say their piece. Not every local
newspaper is going to be interested in their story. And if it were to
become a press issue, the public relations team at whatever social
media platform involved would usually bring out the PR spokesper-
son to save the company's reputation, rather than provide real
support to the victim. The media has an ability to hold tech companies to account, to call them out for their terrible behaviour, and to
bring attention to the realities of what many women and minoritized
communities face. Instead the media are part of the problem.

When you dig deep into the media industry, you see two changes
happening. One, print media is diminishing, making competition
fierce and profit margins razor-thin. It's what's partly led to the
rise of clickbait articles with an unmoderated comments section.
Two, a blog site can instantly become a publishing platform, meaning

we've seen a rise in – and a broadening of what it means to be – journalists, both professional and unprofessional. To make their name, some will get there the only way they feel they can today: through clickbait.

This promotes a savage kind of journalism that ignores the impact it can have on people. Caroline Flack was one tragic victim of this. Caroline was a TV presenter in the UK, and the media took great interest in her personal life. She was constantly hounded by tabloids who wanted to know everything about her love life. Whether Caroline was involved with Prince Harry or One Direction star Harry Styles, the press was always there. She had a history of mental health issues, and had been diagnosed with bipolar disorder not long before her death. In February 2020, Caroline was found dead in her London flat; the cause was suicide. In the aftermath, many British politicians openly condemned the media for their part in the tragedy. One MP, Daisy Cooper, claimed the newspapers had been 'desperate for clickbait'. The situation showed how vicious the press can be, especially when it comes to women's lives. As if they were owed access to the intimate details of Caroline Flack's existence.

The state of journalism

It was Kat Hopps, a journalist, who introduced me to the concept of SEO journalism. She described it to me as a response to topics that are in the news – commenting on what's trending and what's popular. It's an entirely different model of journalism from your feature-led, in-depth reporting. It's a very fast-paced environment; you're working on multiple stories at a time, and as soon as you've finished one story, you're on to the next. You're under so much pressure to keep delivering and putting stories out that you don't think about the consequences of what you've written. Not only for other people, but for yourself as a journalist. You're given tight deadlines, and there isn't much time or space to go into greater depth.

Kat also taught me that a lot of news outlets use a syndicate to pick up stories from a local paper. Syndicated content doesn't give a new or fresh perspective. It purely amplifies the story, and is another comment section for far too many people to be offensive in by masking it as 'just giving their opinion'.

Talking with Kat was an interesting development in my own story. She wrote an article about me that ended up spiralling into another torrent of abuse. When I look back at the situation of the news coverage now, I see it very differently to how I did at the time, now with an understanding of all sides.

I remember this event feeling like a breach of privacy. There I was, not-so-fresh out of the gym and still in my hoodie, just shopping in Morrisons supermarket with my mum. And it was then I was racially profiled.

It was just a weekly shopping trip. The only thing that was different this time was my clothes. We were walking around the aisles, chatting, picking out whatever groceries we needed. As we were finishing up, my mum stepped away to go to the bathroom by the exit as I continued to the car park. That's when a member of staff chased and shouted after me, accusing me of shoplifting. He didn't ask for my receipt, nor was he even a security guard.

I was stunned. Of course I hadn't stolen anything. There was no reason for him to believe I had shoplifted – except for my hoodie and the colour of my skin.

All I could do was go back into the supermarket with him in shock. The entire situation was embarrassing; people were watching in the car park as I was forced to walk back with my shopping. I was mortified, and sat crying in my car after the incident. And, as you do in moments of high emotion, I tweeted without thinking.

That's when I first heard from Kat. She reached out to me for a comment after reading my tweets. At the time, I didn't want a fuss and wanted to be left alone. But she was going to write the story either way; she'd been told to. Begrudgingly, I agreed to give a comment, but at the time, I felt coerced into giving my version of events.

She wanted to give me an opportunity to influence what she wrote in a way that gave me agency. She chose to focus on the fact that I was a councillor wrongfully accused of shoplifting. She left race out of the headline, so as not to bait the racists, instead including it later on in the article to minimize the potential for harm. I agreed to the framing of the original article, because she told me the piece was going to be written anyway. What she didn't tell me – I guess, upon reflection, this was purely down to her being junior in her career and not knowing any better – is that when stories are written by local or national press (depending on the agreement), all the data might be uploaded to a syndicate where anyone else can pick up the story. The *Daily Mail* got hold of it, and they didn't have the same consideration for the placement of my quotes, nor the headline. So eventually my story went viral, just one month after the EU speech.

I'd love to say this was the only time I've had a bad experience with the media, but it's not. In 2020, I was interviewed for *The One Show* as part of a conversation with presenters Matt Baker and Alex Jones about the issue of online abuse. It was around the time the government announced Ofcom would be appointed to regulate social media platforms. It was also the same week as Caroline Flack's passing.

Rehearsals that afternoon went well. Then we went live, and Alex Jones mispronounced my name in a big way. When you have an uncommon name, it happens a lot. I have a very expressive face. In the interview, not only can you see that I'm visibly shocked, the camera cuts perfectly to a close-up of my face. Moments after coming off-air, my reaction became a GIF on Twitter.

At first it was an amusing meme. There were strangers from around the world having fun with this GIF of me in a situation they all recognized. It was simply strangers with a 'unique' name bonding over a similar lived experience. It was unifying and funny. Then, out of nowhere, the *Daily Mirror* printed an article sensationalizing the situation, pitting Alex Jones and me against one another. They used a still from video of the interview to convey the most aggressively rude expression.

After Alex Jones's apology at 3.30 p.m., the 'story' was over and done. But by 9 p.m., the *Daily Mirror* had chosen to print fictional beef for clickbait. Not only did the *Daily Mirror* put us both in vulnerable positions, they distracted us from important topics – trading a discussion of suicide, the campaign #bekind and online abuse for clickbait.

Instead of asking for a direct quote and the real story, the young female journalist had – as I understand it now – picked up on the incident from social media, twisting and amplifying it. She made me out to be aggressive. And to top it all off, the *Daily Mirror* left their comments section open and unmonitored.

Not only was there no consideration for my safety in how the article was written and then shared with an unmonitored comments section, but my opinion was never asked for – taking away my agency. Plus there were adverts **all** over the article. The amount of money being made off the back of clickbait is insane. It wasn't written for me or raising awareness of the 'wrongdoing', as she claimed. It was written from a sensationalist perspective, all for clicks and profit. They knew what they were doing, and had no qualms about me being collateral damage.

Removing context

When I talked to Yassmin Abdel-Magied about this, she had a similar story that showed how even the most innocuous comments can get taken out of context. She'd once sat down and done an interview with a newspaper in Australia, and had mentioned once in this hour-and-a-half session that, at one point in time, she had wanted to be a Formula 1 driver. Alas, she said to the reporter, she had gone down a different path in life. But when the article went live, it did so with the headline 'Fired up to be the first female, Muslim F1 driver'. Out of the entire interview, that was the nugget they chose to be the focus. It was harmless enough, but it showed Yassmin how the media can easily dictate the discussions being had about you. After that, she would be asked constantly about how her Formula 1 career was going.

And while this example might be a funny story, Yassmin has had other experiences with the media that haven't gone so well. 'In my transition to becoming persona non grata in Australia, the fuss was that I walked out of a panel,' she told me. 'A well-renowned American author came to my home city of Brisbane for a writers' festival and opened her talk with a discussion about how cultural appropriation was a fad. And she was wearing a sombrero; it was a whole thing. I was sitting at the front with my mum and, as I was sitting there – one of the few writers of colour in the audience – everyone was laughing at her jokes. I turned to my mum and said I couldn't sit there and listen to it. So I walked out.

'The next day, I came back to the festival and talked to others who didn't see the problem with what she had said. They thought it was fine. So I decided I needed to write something; I wrote a blog post. This was republished by the *Guardian* (with my permission) and it blew up. I didn't know who this author was, or how big a deal she was. Everyone freaked out. It blew up the literary world to the extent that, six months later, at another writers' festival in India, I bumped into a guy exclaiming, "You're the one they're all afraid of!" I got a month's worth of hate mail and messages on Twitter and Facebook. But because it was confined to the literary world, it was a smaller story.'

Unfortunately, Yassmin would also learn how it feels to be part of a bigger story. Earlier in this book, I mentioned her experience of appearing on a debate show, the Australian equivalent of *Question Time*. She had her own viral video situation, and the media was quick to pick up on it. But instead of talking to her and getting her side of the story, they painted her as someone who consulted with terror-ists. Yassmin thought the story would go away, but time and time again, the press kept coming back to her. Yassmin's colleague calculated that over 220,000 words were written about her during this time.

'I think the fallout from the three events – the article about walk-ing out of the talk, the viral video of my debate and a seven-word Facebook post on Anzac Day that I almost immediately deleted and apologized for – fundamentally altered the tenor of my relationships with everyone in my life,' she said. 'My relationship with my parents has never been as close, because they didn't know how to deal with what had happened, and I found the experience excruciatingly isolat-ing as a result. It shattered something in my family. I left the country. I have never wanted anything to do with it since. I've thought a lot about giving up my Australian citizenship. Because what does it mean to belong somewhere if that's what happens to you? If the state itself participates in your public destruction. I was made an example of, you know, [and] getting "Yassmined" is now an academically rec-ognized term for what happens if a woman of colour steps out of line in the press.'

There's more to journalism than misreporting and dramatizing situations. That's just lazy journalism. But that laziness has become acceptable. So how can the media step up and be better?

Risk assessments

To make the media environment safe for all people, journalists need to be completing risk assessments before presenting their subjects' stories. Too often, people – especially women and those from minoritized communities – are unwillingly made the star. And the media will write about them without considering what effect this might have on their lives. Even something funny and innocuous can draw people's hate.

Imagine you're walking down the street, acting silly for your mates who are recording you on their phones. You're not looking and – oops – you accidentally walk into a pole. Your friends burst out laughing and, not seriously injured, you join in. The person recording it uploads it to their Instagram so you can relive it later on, and that's that. A hilarious story between friends. But someone outside your group of friends sees it, and they share it around, and before you know it, you've gone viral. Before long, a media outlet picks up on it and writes a fluff piece so they can tick off another article submitted. This is then shared with their hundreds of thousands of followers worldwide, and then it's open season for criticism. To make matters worse, journalists include your full name and other personal details, making it much easier for people to find you. The comment section is rife with microaggressions you have no control over. Shots are fired and the media outlet gets paid, while you get propelled unwillingly into the spotlight, vulnerable and unprotected.

The media outlet doesn't care about the person in the video; they care about their bottom line. But the story has an adverse effect on the person in question. If the outlet had completed a risk assessment, they would have realized that they were putting someone who could be easily identified in a position where they could be attacked.

This is magnified for anybody talking about topics such as social justice and human rights. We can be mindful that journalists are doing their job, but equally journalists should consider that the 'characters' in their stories are real people. Because this wasn't considered when the *Daily Mirror* and *Daily Mail* picked up my story, I was getting abused again. And because it wasn't considered in Yassmin's case, she was practically run out of the country that was her home. There are consequences to publishing these stories, and the media needs to realize that. This is an opportunity for journalism to be creative within the principles of responsible journalism – to creatively address identified risks. This might mean agreeing to moderate comments on socials and the website – or even offering to turn comments off. And it might mean using a pseudonym or avoiding tagging personal social media accounts – or at least gaining consent.

Accountability

What's missing from the press and media is accountability. Newspapers can run front-page stories that drag someone, but can get away with it by including a small column on page 16 the next day retracting anything contentious they said.

This is all part and parcel with the fact we've become accustomed to a twenty-four-hour news cycle. We never used to be that way. We would wait until we were sitting cross-legged in front of the nine o'clock news. Now we're plugged into the system constantly, and that's not good for us. Is it any wonder there's so much pressure to create news, and that the quality of it is so low?

It's up to the bigwigs at the top to create a better process for reporting news, but this can't be just at one outlet, it needs to be unanimous. Part of this is making sure these media outlets are taken to task for irresponsible journalism. They do what they do because they are allowed to get away with it. And not everyone has the cultural capital to challenge them and force them to retract any lies.

Where media accountability will come from is twofold. First, the public needs to call them out. Whether you take to Twitter, Facebook or even Instagram, it's worth making your voice heard. Will it make a huge difference? Well, it isn't likely to change the way of the world overnight, but the more people do it, and the more people see it, the greater the chance of change happening. Second, governments need to step in and encourage this new way of reporting. Regulation of the media hasn't caught up with the fast-paced social media landscape, and the government needs to regulate how journalists can talk about people.

End the silence

The media also needs to stand with the victims of online abuse publicly. And not just the abuse of Hollywood celebrities, but everyday women and minority groups who are disproportionately affected and are raising awareness of this harm. The more they magnify these public stories – responsibly and consensually – the greater the chance that we can begin to stamp out this behaviour. Granted this is a difficult balance to achieve, but that shouldn't be used to justify silence. With many media platforms being nationwide, if not international, they have a lot of influence and power. To have their voices in our corner can be highly effective.

In 2020, Channel 4 teamed up with Nationwide Building Society (and other large companies) to run a powerful #TogetherAgainst-Hate campaign in the UK. This was in support of customer-facing staff who regularly faced abuse. To have one of the main TV networks in the country run a nationwide campaign against hate was refreshing to see, and showed people that this kind of behaviour can't be tolerated.

Moderating comments

Part of the issue is how often media platforms let online abuse run rampant on their websites. It would be slightly less frustrating if newspapers spoke up about how they will not tolerate any of the hateful comments. But more often than not, they stay quiet and let the hate fester.

Media platforms have the power to moderate these comments or remove them entirely. They can even go as far as banning abusive users from commenting again. But most of them don't, for similar reasons tech companies don't. Engagement earns them money. If they have angry people typing up a storm of hateful bigotry, they have engaged customers. Ones who will come back again and again to make their voices heard. The media feed this habit by writing more controversial stories.

What outlets need to do is put their foot down and be stricter with their comment moderation. Especially on stories concerning women and minoritized communities. They could even close the comments on those stories altogether.

What next?

This lack of care and attention from the media and news outlets is why it's so important to create boundaries and maintain control of your agency, which we will discuss in upcoming chapters. You have to be in control of your media profile, your storytelling and online interactions as much as possible, because if one journalist thinks something you've done or that has happened to you is going to be a source of entertainment or a career-making story, you're instantly put at increased risk of abuse.

This isn't me bashing individual journalists, as they aren't thinking of the risks at the time. The fast-paced nature of their role and the industry doesn't allow them room to consider your vulnerabilities.

Perpetrators

> *Don't drive drunk and don't tweet upset, both seriously screw up your judgement and response time.*
>
> Zelda Williams, Twitter, October 2021

Who or what can be a perpetrator of online abuse is vast. As I see it, there are two types: those who don't realize they feed into the system, and those who cause harm on purpose. These are 'unconscious' and 'conscious' perpetrators respectively. So what separates the two?

Unconscious perpetrators

Unconscious perpetrators are usually those who are caught up in the moment. As youngers would say, they're lost in the 'banter'. They're likely to be completely oblivious to the impact their action may have, or what it might do in combination with tens of others. They're trapped in an environment that's perpetuating some sort of viral abuse, and they haven't taken the time to self-reflect and consider the impact. Algorithms on social media platforms fuel this fire as if it were a competitive sport. They lock us into echo chambers – online spaces where all we hear are people with the same opinions as us. We throw around jokes, thinking they're acceptable because, in that community, they are. But we rarely consider the people we're aiming at. I'm not saying we're being purposefully spiteful in these instances. We just don't realize what we're doing.

Meme culture often blurs these boundaries. You use images or GIFs of people in certain emotional states to make a joke about how you're feeling. It's harmless – you don't do it with any malicious intent. But there's a story behind those memes.

I see a lot of memes of Black people frantically crying or exceptionally sad paired with something 'funny' written over the top. A lot of the time there is a deeper backstory, they're acting that way because they've lost somebody or they're trying to get help for something. Do we ever stop to think about how this person feels, constantly seeing their face out there? It's a perpetual reminder of when they were at their lowest point. Did they give consent for the image to be shared? Has anyone asked them how they feel?

Who are the key players in online abuse, and what can they do differently?

It's a difficult subject, because it's such a fine line. This isn't about censorship and being afraid to be playful. It's about asking where the banter starts and ends. Once we start to recognize that fine line and catch ourselves, we can stop being a part of the problem.

Status updates are another space where there's minimal time to reflect; they're instant. When you open Facebook, the first question you're asked is 'What's on your mind?' It's incentivizing you to speak without thinking. And that's exactly what too many people do online. Most of the time, it's harmless and nothing comes of it. But it's not the platforms that have to live with the repercussions – it's you. You have to take responsibility for your own words. Someone can pull out your accidental wrongdoing at any time once it's live, because screenshots and your digital footprint are eternal as far as the web is concerned – far beyond the time you spent thinking about it.

Take Chrissy Teigen, for example. Infamous as Twitter's biggest unwitting troll, her social media career mainly consisted of shots fired, a sharp tongue and a carefree, one-of-the-lads approach. But the reality of a lot of her content was that she ended up attacking a fair few people with her supposedly light-hearted posts. It took accountability knocking at her door for her to realize the impact of her actions, and she issued a public apology on Instagram in June 2021 after she was accused of bullying:

> Not a day, not a single moment has passed where I haven't felt the crushing weight of regret for the things I've said in the past . . .
>
> There is simply no excuse for my past horrible tweets. My targets didn't deserve them. No one does. Many of them needed empathy, kindness, understanding and support, not my meanness masquerading as a kind of casual, edgy humor.
>
> I was a troll, full stop. And I am so sorry.

I'm not defending any of the comments she made in the past. She addressed the problem herself. Many of her posts were attempts at humour, but a human being was hurt for the sake of a few likes. And we all have the potential to create this environment when we don't think about what we're saying before we press send.

We don't even have to be saying anything negative. Something written or sent with the best of intentions can have negative effects. In 2021, actor Jamie Costa went viral for a video where he portrayed the late Robin Williams during his *Mork & Mindy* days. And he was **good** – almost scarily accurate. For many people, I imagine it was comforting seeing this icon brought back to life. In their excitement, some sent it to Zelda Williams, Robin's daughter. Maybe they thought she would find similar comfort in it. But she didn't, and rightfully so. It must have been painful for her to have to be confronted with this unasked-for reminder of her dad. So she tweeted: 'Jamie is SUPER talented, this isn't against him, but y'all spamming me an impression of my late dad on one of his saddest days is weird.' No one was in the wrong here. But the situation demonstrated how we need to be aware of how our actions might affect others.

No one is perfect. But unconscious perpetrators have a great capacity for change and therefore for changing our online culture. Often, I refer to myself as a 'recovering dickhead'. People have hurt me and I've taken to the internet at various times and said something I've later regretted. I had wise friends and room to grow; to recognize when my actions were wrong. And with some self-reflection and effort, I became a better person.

The reality is that many of you will be an occasional unconscious perpetrator without realizing it. I'm not here to scold you for that. But now you're aware of how your actions might be inflicting harm on others, you can join me in the recovering dickhead club, make better choices and become a better digital citizen to those around you. Here are some things you can do.

Give yourself time to think

Before you send that tweet, post that status update or make that comment, take a step back. There's this pressure to post right **now**, almost like an algorithmic peer pressure. By giving yourself time to think about what you really want to say, you can reflect on your words. Ask yourself if they have the potential to hurt anyone. Are you being needlessly callous? Is there a human being involved? Are you perpetuating microaggressions? Giving yourself this space to reflect can also help you organize your thoughts and realize how you really feel about a situation.

Don't post at all

Part of this reflection may result in you realizing you don't have to post. It's like that old expression: if you don't have anything nice to say, don't say anything at all. We can all have an opinion on the current hot topic, like Kim Kardashian's latest Instagram post, but do we always have to leave our hypercritical opinions in the comments?

Why are you posting?

Sometimes, we post with the best intentions, but ultimately it's still all about us and our ego. Say you take to the streets to give a homeless person some money or a sandwich. You take a selfie with the person and post it with a caption like, 'This isn't for me, this is to inspire others to do the same.' But there are so many other ways to inspire action. Instead of 'leading by example' for the likes, share resources and impactful stats from organizations educating on the cause you're passionate about.

And these are just some of the ways real and systemic change can be inspired. Whenever you're sharing content you haven't curated, aim to get permission and signpost and tag them or their organization/campaign. Be critical of why you're posting something, and ask yourself if you're coming at it with the best intentions.

Social media superiority complex

Many of us have grown up with the internet **and** in a society that holds archaic beliefs – patriarchy and white supremacy being two of the biggest culprits. From an early age, we're constantly sent a bunch of signals reinforcing divisive and harmful stereotypes of gender, race, sexuality and more. But thanks to civil liberation campaigns, relationship and sex education, decolonizing work, and frameworks like feminism and queer theory, we have the opportunity to be more enlightened than the generations before us. Literature, entertainment and activism provoke thought and encourage education – highlighting key issues to get us to think, feel and know differently about a subject. We have school and university debates all about changing our opponents' minds. And social media platforms make vital education even easier to access, with a growing number of educational accounts posting on important topics of today – such as race, trans rights, and conflicts in the Global South.

Yet, despite the fact we're all learning as we go, when it comes to the online space we now expect people to be woke as soon as they create their social media accounts.

For those of us who grew up on forums and social media platforms, our digital footprints can make it even harder to dissociate from rejected archaic beliefs. Undoing the social conditioning of patriarchy, racism and all forms of oppression within the ninety seconds of choosing a first profile photo is a mighty ask. Now, to be clear, this doesn't mean people have free rein to be abusive or bigoted online. But there's a growing conflict within online spaces, and it requires nuanced discussions.

How many of us truly understand the impact of our digital footprint? Or that we don't get to take words back from the online space? The social norms for how to behave online are an ongoing project (and some would argue we've not achieved this offline either), yet we are reprimanding adults for their behaviour from when they were teens. And all this in a world where Holocaust denial and the use of dehumanizing language was not banned by Facebook until 2020.

Of course, there's an argument that being racist or sexist as a teen cannot simply be dismissed as an experiment or a phase someone went through. How long will women and minoritized communities continue to be a topic that people 'experiment' with? My answer to that is: as long as we fail to invest in and commit to decolonizing our education.

We find ourselves in a world where we have to actively consider, or plan for, deleting our previous social media posts. But does this just perpetuate a culture that expects perfection from our young people – something that is in direct conflict with our human fallibility? This is something Jameela Jamil brought up in our interview: 'No one has the right to tell you when you're done learning. When you're done growing. No one else is allowed to tell you when your time is up. I refuse. That is only for you to decide.'

This conflict is amplified by algorithms and bad actors. But it's also, in my opinion, amplified by a superiority complex. It's a game of virtue signalling online, and showing off as the better ally. It's dangerous, because a lot of this unlearning and re-education through books, talks and listening needs to be done not just online, but offline too. The gatekeeping and expectation of perfection intimidates people trying to learn and blocks them from accessing the information they need.

I witnessed this intensely after George Floyd's murder. The world was taking a (much-needed) basic course on anti-Blackness and racism. Yet some used this as an opportunity to point, poke, expose and call out those who were behind on the journey. Those who weren't consumed by a state of urgency to post a statement while they were taking the time to understand the matter. In spring 2021, as the world was learning about the growing violence in Israel and Palestine, a well-known influencer woke up to abusive direct messages on Instagram because she hadn't posted about something that had happened the night before. It's also true that women face more scrutiny online, are held to a much higher standard for their past and present online behaviour, and are routinely 'exposed', 'blackmailed' and 'leaked'.

The culture of instant gratification cannot apply to learning. Can we be real? There will be many of you reading these pages that, at some point in your life, have said something online or offline that has been to the detriment of, or caused harm to, someone else. I know I have. No one's perfect, but it's about what you do with the knowledge you now have. We need more celebrities like Chrissy Teigen apologizing for being abusive in the past and changing their behaviour going forward.

We need to accept that some people will have written awful things in the past. What we need to be concerned with is authentic behavioural change. It's simply arrogance to think we've learned all we can.

Conscious perpetrators

Then you have the people who go out of their way to cause harm. The racists, the women- or men-haters, the transphobic and homophobic, the people that think being able-bodied makes them better than others. They actively go out to cause suffering. They'll join communities on platforms and use mob-style trolling tactics to make people's lives miserable. They'll go on to the pages of the trans community or jump on social justice and liberation hashtags, knowing they'll find their desired targets. They're the people you see mentioning #BlackLivesMatter or #AsianLivesMatter in an attempt to derail the conversation and cause anarchy.

There have even been cases of people pretending to be BLM activists to make money and fundraise while never contributing to the cause. The biggest page on Facebook that claimed to be part of the BLM movement was a scam. This middle-aged white man in

Australia was running a page with almost 700,000 followers. That was twice as many as the **official** Black Lives Matter page had at the time. Of the $100,000 raised, at least some of it was transferred to a personal bank account, not the actual cause that could have benefited from those critical funds.

Incels are another example. These online communities believe society is hierarchized according to sexual attractiveness. They therefore blame women for subjugating them to an inferior existence and 'forcing' them into celibacy. Online, this manifests as endless hate and abuse targeted towards women. A vast array of communities all spurring each other on to punish women by any means possible.

In 2021, streaming site Twitch faced a new trend known as 'hate raiding'. Raiding was already a feature on the platform. Content creators could send their audience to 'raid' a friend's stream when they were finished. Everyone would pile into the new stream, and bring it some views. But hate raiding is for more sinister reasons. Using bots and fake accounts, hate raids specifically target women, LGBTQIA+ and racial minority streamers, filling their chat boxes with hateful rhetoric. By the time the streamer can shut it down, the damage is done. They've seen the hate.

Unfortunately, in these instances – where people know their online behaviour is abuse and will cause harm – I don't believe education will ever be enough. Which is exactly why we need to implement stronger moderation and legislation.

A public health approach enables us to look at why people are becoming perpetrators in the first place. Is it the spreading of misinformation? Social inequality? Loneliness? Isolation? Poor education? A lack of communication and healthy conversation? Overcrowding? A lack of mental health services? No discrimination is ever okay, but what's causing it in the first place? Often, perpetrators were once victims, and their victims might go on to become perpetrators themselves. As a result, we create a cycle of violence where everyone is hurting one another – and, without intervention, it's going to continue.

But until we can reach out to them, educate and enable them to have a more positive relationship with the online space, we need to work towards reducing conscious perpetrators' platforms and limiting their opportunities to do harm. On the individual level, this looks like building up our digital self-care and defence tools to counter those who go out of their way to cause harm. We don't stop ourselves from going out into the world because we know there are bad people out there. The same applies online. We don't have to personally stop using online spaces to avoid these behaviours, but we can make intentional changes to ensure as consumers and members of the online space we're not rewarding or glamourizing online abuse. We can set our standards as to what type of digital citizen we want to be, and who we want to allow into our space. We can actively create a safer online space for ourselves.

To put it simply, perpetrators are out there. We don't need to give them too much room to breathe – we know they exist. They're people choosing to do bad things, but we shouldn't have to live our lives overwhelmed by anxiety about those trying to hurt us. If we develop appropriate legislation, create new positive social norms and educate on what online abuse looks like, how to deal with it and how not to be a part of it, then we can thrive.

The next step? Equipping ourselves with the knowledge we need. It's time to build our digital self-care toolkit.

Chapter Five: Building your digital self-care toolkit

Honestly, we need to start thinking of muting, blocking, and reporting as the seatbelts of safety for digital platforms.

Caroline Sinders, Twitter, July 2021

A quote from Queen B Beyoncé herself offers a helpful initiation into the topic of self-care. In an interview with *Harper's Bazaar* in September 2021, she explained an approach that resonated a lot with me and my evolving relationship with the online space.

When asked how she processes the changing world of celebrity culture and protects her inner self, she explained:

> We live in a world with few boundaries and a lot of access. There are so many internet therapists, comment critics, and experts with no expertise. Our reality can be warped because it's based on a personalized algorithm . . . It's easy to forget that there's still so much to discover outside of our phones. I'm grateful I have the ability to choose what I want to share. One day I decided I wanted to be like Sade and Prince . . . My music, my films, my art, my message – that should be enough.
>
> Throughout my career, I've been intentional about setting boundaries between my stage persona and my personal life . . . I've surrounded myself with honest people who I admire, who have their own lives and dreams and are not dependent on me . . . A lot of who I am is reserved for the people I love and

> trust . . . *Trust, the reason those folks don't see certain things*
> *about me is because my Virgo ass does not want them to see*
> *it . . . It's not because it doesn't exist!*

Community, boundaries, commitment, intention, reflections –
these are things Beyoncé has found are important in developing
self-care. But whether you're an icon trying to maintain some sense
of privacy and normalcy, or an everyday digital citizen trying to strike
the healthiest and happiest balance between being online and pre-
serving your sanity, a lot of the same guidance rings true.

Let's explore how we can apply this approach online, with digital
self-care.

Introducing digital self-care

Self-care is something that's often forgotten about when we talk
about online abuse and safety. We change our bras, check for lumps,
wash our hair and have regular routines in our offline lives. But we
have to make self-care part of our online routine too. To increase
our resilience and ability to overcome online negativity and hate, and
to keep ourselves sane in an online world that seems to be constantly out for blood.

To put it simply, the ultimate goal of digital self-care is to forge a
healthier relationship with online platforms and technology. To take
up space more safely and confidently online. To empower yourself
to harness the incredible potential of online communities for whatever it is you're passionate about and want to achieve.

Digital self-care means noticing when you need to rest and take a
break from existing online. It means saying no to others and saying
yes to yourself and your own needs. It's setting boundaries. It's asking for help. It's saving for therapy. It's weighing up the pros and cons
of engaging with others and sometimes refusing to take part in

public life – full stop. It's building a personalized toolkit, affirming boundaries and regularly checking in with yourself, **especially** after a traumatic experience. It's non-negotiable self-love in the face of so much negativity and harm.

Digital self-care is also about understanding online abuse and how it can cause trauma. Which is what we've been working on up to this point. We've spent plenty of time looking at the scope of what online abuse is, and exploring the context in which online abuse is currently thriving. Now we need to use this knowledge to better protect and empower ourselves. Remember that you have agency. You are responsible – not for the abuse, but for your behaviours, thoughts, reactions and interactions when it comes to technology and others. You can make a conscious choice to seek out joyful content, as well as create joyful content yourself.

Sadly, there isn't a one-size-fits-all method of self-care. We live in a world where we are always seeking a shortcut. What one thing can we do today to fix this? But there isn't a way to fix online violence or its impacts in one fell swoop. It will be slightly different for everyone. And what works one day might not work another. It requires practice and an ongoing commitment.

Tool 1: Intentions and values

Ask yourself how *you* want to exist online. How public do you want to be? Are certain accounts going to be exclusively personal and others public? How will you – and won't you – tolerate being treated online? What are your guiding principles for how you treat others?

This is a necessary first step. By sitting down and setting out your intentions and values, you can get a firm grasp on what your time spent online should look like. It allows you to set strict boundaries around what you are and aren't willing to accept. And from there, it becomes a lot easier to recognize when situations start to veer off course and slip into grey areas.

Outlining what your intentions and values are also gives you a benchmark so you can regularly check in on your security and privacy settings. By setting the standards by which you'll exist online, you begin to take back some of the power and ownership of your time on the World Wide Web.

Now, let's break this process down a little bit further.

What is this account for?

For every account you currently have, and for any future ones you might create, you want to be super clear on what your intentions are. Ideally, you set these before you establish the account, but it's not too late to do this for all the ones you currently have.

It's important to clarify here what I mean by an 'account'. This could be social media, email, subscriptions, memberships – or anything you have to log into. To keep it simple I'll focus on social media accounts, as they're where you're more likely to run into online abuse, but most of this advice can be applied across the board.

My advice is to:

- Make a list of all the platforms you use.
- Next to each, write down why you use it.
- Is it purely for escapism and entertainment, like aimlessly scrolling through your Instagram feed?
- Or do you use it for engaging in healthy, productive online discussion, such as on Twitter or Reddit?

These are just a couple of examples. You might also use a platform for career progression, keeping up with current affairs, getting your entertainment news, a sense of community or to promote your own work. Whatever the reason, note it down.

For each platform, you then want to ask yourself whether you're getting the intended benefits. If Instagram is meant to be your go-to for light-hearted entertainment but you're coming away feeling even worse than when you opened the app, that's a tell-tale sign that something needs to change. Similarly, if opening Reddit drags you into a toxic pack mentality and a whirlwind of abuse, it might be time to find somewhere else for healthy discussions.

Working out your purpose for each platform allows you to be more considered and self-aware of how you're existing online. Clarifying what each account is for not only helps focus the time and energy you spend online, it also allows you to see where there are any personal security risks.

How public do you want to be?

A big part of being online is deciding what you want to be public knowledge and what you would prefer to keep private. Which parts of yourself and your life do you want to be online? What information do you want people to have access to? In most cases, privacy controls are automatically set to the most public options, meaning you can show up on search engines. So you need to clearly define those lines: what do you want people to know, and what do you want them **not** to know?

A part of this is assessing how your choices impact those around you. For example, if I took my relationship online, it's not only me who could face abuse. My boyfriend could quickly become a target too. In the past, photos of my own mother and grandmother were used in an article because I had family images online. The pictures were from what I had naively thought was my personal Instagram, but a *Daily Mail* journalist brought them into a very public space for everyone to see and comment on, for an article that my family had nothing to do with. That was a painful lesson that if my Instagram account isn't set to private, then everything is up for grabs.

Any account that shares aspects of your personal life or daily whereabouts deserves more attention in terms of security and privacy. Or at least some careful consideration as to what you're posting and when. Give particular thought to apps or forums that access your location – such as Strava or the Nike Run Club App, which track your physical activity and where you've been. By staying in control of what you keep public and private – by making sure it's **your** choice – you minimize the power you're giving away to others.

With public-facing, professional accounts, you'll probably create different boundaries than you do for personal ones. After all, if you're serving as an extension of a brand or institution, there are associated reputational and financial risks to consider.

Social media doesn't have to blend your personal and professional lives. To stay safer online, why not create separate accounts for your public role, and use a nickname or alias for your personal accounts? You can have varying degrees of privacy on each – so, if you want, you can keep your private life private while still maintaining a public presence.

If you do opt for hybrid accounts that blend your professional and personal lives, you're going to want to clearly identify where you draw the line. What boundaries can you set around your online engagement?

You don't have to be bullied out of not sharing aspects of yourself online, but it's worth being aware of your presence. Privacy settings are your friend. Of course, if you *want* to share everything under the sun, then that's your choice and you should go for it. All I'm encouraging you to do is to take some extra time to reflect beforehand.

Discriminatory comments targeting an aspect of your identity rely on people being able to comment in the first place. If you're open about your identity online, which you have every right to be, you also have the option to minimize peoples' opportunity to have a say. Some platforms, such as Instagram, have the functionality to turn off comments on your posts, so now is the time to consider what restrictions you want to put on others' access to your accounts.

What are your guiding values and principles?

Think of your guiding values and principles as your personal code of conduct for the online space. How do you want to exist as an online citizen? How do you want to be treated? And to what standard do you hold your treatment of others?

When I spoke to human rights lawyer Adam Wagner, he shared his personal rules for engaging online:

1. *Don't insult people* – Don't go after the person. (Sub-rule: Never say anything you wouldn't want your mum, children or a judge to see.)
2. *Be honest* – Try not to be too proud if you come to realize your opinion is wrong. Integrity is important. It's okay to show your working out in public, and to document your journey from one perspective to another.
3. *You can't win* – It's naive to think you can ever win an argument with a random stranger on Twitter. Communicate with the people who are listening to you, not the people who are arguing with you. And model the behaviour that fits with the answer. You can't talk about human rights, dignity or empathy unless you're showing those qualities yourself.

Take some time to consider the person you do and don't want to be online. Write your own set of guiding rules if it's helpful.

Remember, equally important to identifying your online values and principles is holding yourself accountable when it comes to following through. Check in with yourself regularly, and reflect on whether you've been living by your code of conduct on different platforms. If you have, great. If you haven't, don't beat yourself up. Show yourself some grace and compassion, and identify ways to do better moving forward.

NEVER USE
SOCIAL MEDIA TO
VALIDATE
YOUR EXISTENCE.
PEOPLE CAN
LIKE YOU
WITHOUT
LIKING
YOUR POSTS,
AND VICE VERSA.
LOVE
IS NOT DIGITAL,
AND YOU
MUST NOT
WAIT FOR LIKES,
TO LIKE YOURSELF.

Vex King, Instagram, 2021

Tool 2: Reflection and check-ins

Continual learning is critical. Over time, you take information from your environment and draw lessons from it. And you're not always going to get it right! It's why you have to have compassion for yourself. Self-care is about accepting that you aren't perfect, that you can grow, and that you still deserve love in spite of that. You're a work in progress, and that's great.

Never be too harsh on yourself. That's a pitfall for many. They turn inwards and become self-critical if they get something wrong. Don't let that happen; show yourself some grace. You can also turn learning into a collaborative process. What can you learn from others? What do their experiences tell you? Maintain a willingness to expand your views.

Taking time to check in with yourself allows you to analyse what's happening. In the moment, it can be difficult to comprehend why you might act a certain way. But if you give yourself the space to think about it, you might find what triggered you and why. From here, you can work on a much healthier response, giving you more control over your life.

Honour how you feel

When it comes to existing online, it's important to listen to your body and honour how you feel. To trust in your intuition, and know when to react to a negative comment – and when to switch off your phone and conserve your energy.

Mamta Saha shared with me how she encourages her clients to set boundaries for themselves and prioritize internal, reflective work when it comes to experiencing negativity online or simply *feeling* negative online: 'I think it's important to understand your purpose. "Why am I going online? And what's my intention?" And then duration of time. So create that picket fence around the time that you're going to spend on there . . . And notice your thoughts and feelings as

IF YOU'RE TOO BUSY
GETTING TRIGGERED,
YOU WON'T HAVE ADEQUATE TIME AND ENERGY TO
DISCOVER WHY.
YOU NEED UNHINDERED SPACE TO
QUESTION,
REFLECT,
AND REWRITE
OLD AND UNHELPFUL PATTERNS . . .
SUPPOSE YOU USE ANONYMOUS/SECRET ACCOUNTS
TO KEEP AN EYE ON
PEOPLE YOU DISLIKE,
OR TO TARGET THEM
WHEN THE OPPORTUNITY ARISES.
IN THAT CASE, YOU'RE
LITERALLY WAITING
TO BE TRIGGERED OR TO
DISPLAY HATE.
EMBRACING ENERGY THAT IS UNHELPFUL OR
UNCONSTRUCTIVE WILL KEEP YOU IN A
WEB OF NEGATIVITY.

Vex King, Instagram

you're scrolling. "How does this make me feel? Whose Insta stories am I avoiding?" It's listening to yourself, paying attention to that internal narrative. That's going to give you lots of cues. And I think when we start to do that, to honour how we feel, we adapt as opposed to reacting to what's going on. You respond authentically. You notice, "Okay, that doesn't feel good. I don't want to watch that person's Stories. I'm going to unfollow."

'It's taking this as an opportunity to look at "What is this teaching me about me? Why is this triggering and what can I do within myself to heal this body?" . . . It's about looking at oneself. Because I do think we live in a world now where it's so easy to point the finger or call somebody out. But there's a real growth opportunity there within ourselves. Which isn't easy to evolve but, if we do, it makes us that bit stronger and builds our armour to be able to not be threatened. We know ourselves better.'

Checking in with yourself

So what does it mean to 'check in' with yourself? It's about being aware of how you change in certain situations online. This might be looking at how your energy shifts when scrolling through different content. Or how your body reacts to content you don't like. How's your breathing? Can you feel yourself holding tension in your body?

Checking in requires you to look at where you are both mentally and physically. What can you do in the moment to ground yourself? Can you do it on your own, or do you need help? Do the people you follow bring you joy, or do they make you feel shit? If following certain people is no longer additive to your life, hit that unfollow button and protect your peace. And remember, as you grow and change, so will your boundaries. So review them regularly.

When you feel yourself going to a dark place, that's when you need to check in the most!

WHEN POSTING,
IT'S IMPORTANT TO
REMEMBER
IT'S NOT THE
RESPONSIBILITY
OF STRANGERS
ON THE INTERNET TO
MAKE YOU
FEEL SAFE
OR CATER TO YOUR
INDIVIDUAL EXPERIENCE.
ALTER THEMSELVES
TO MAKE YOU FEEL
MORE COMFORTABLE.
VALIDATE YOU.
ANYTHING ELSE YOU DEMAND OF THEM.
THEY ARE STRANGERS.
ON THE INTERNET.

Seerut K. Chawla, Instagram, 2021

Questions to ask yourself

When looking at your online presence and what you view every day, it's worth regularly asking yourself what is and isn't working. This involves some soul-searching about your feelings and what effects different content has on you. For this, you need to be brutally honest, be kind to yourself, and dig into what's harmful to you.

For all the feeds from the social media apps you're on, every news or entertainment website, every comment section, ask yourself if it's adding value to your life. Do you come away from it feeling enriched in some way? Like you've learned something valuable, important? The benefits should outweigh the costs, and you should never come away from an online space feeling worse.

Does certain content make you a better, more informed and more empathetic digital citizen? If not, consider why you would want to keep it around. Of course, not all content is about betterment; some of it is about joy. Does the content that is meant to make you feel happy or laugh do its job?

Are you comparing yourself to others? Comparison is a thief of joy. While you should always strive to be a better person, you can't judge yourself by the progress of others. Their journeys are not yours. And change is a long-term process; don't be harsh on yourself because you decide to take time off.

Regularly asking yourself these questions will help you to realize how you're feeling in the moment, and where you can make your online experience a more positive one. Find the balance in your online space, and stay focused on your own path.

Making mistakes

If you do make a mistake and cross a line with somebody, reflect on how you can be better. Other people will have boundaries of their own, and you have to acknowledge when you're in the wrong. If you ever do this, reach out with a real apology.

Word it carefully; they might not be open to talking just yet. And that's their right. Just tell them that you see where you went wrong and what you've learned from the situation. In time, you can heal your relationship and rebuild bridges.

Tool 3: A proactive mindset

A big part of your digital self-care toolkit is being proactive. Reacting to the online abuse or harm you're currently facing is vital, but preventing yourself from facing it in the first place (where possible) is just as crucial.

Most women do this offline because we've learned from a young age that it's the safest course of action. 'Thanks' to the patriarchal society in which we live, there are ways women have been conditioned to navigate offline spaces. We don't jog alone at night. Where possible, we arrange to be picked up from a well-lit train station after a night out. We have our phones primed and ready to record any incidents on public transport. We don't leave our drinks unattended when in bars or nightclubs.

Sadly, it would be remiss of me not to acknowledge that we can be doing all of this – and take a whole host of measures to minimize the risks of our patriarchal society – and still be attacked. For example, drug-facilitated rape cases. Or cases like those of Sarah Everard – murdered by a police officer – and sisters Bibaa and Nicole – murdered by a complete stranger – amongst plenty of others.

It's frustrating that we have to do all this proactive work offline, and it's even more infuriating that we have to start doing it online too. As we've mastered it in one form, now it's about transferring those 'street smarts' into a new arena.

A big part of digital self-care starts with your mindset. When you enter the online space, remember you're opening yourself up to **everyone** in the world, not just people you know. When you leave a public comment on, let's say a friend's photo, you are not the only two people in the room, there are several witnesses. Or say you have a public account and tweet that same person, everyone in the world has access to your innermost thoughts.

When I started out on Twitter, I naively thought, 'I'm tweeting to my political party friends. I'm tweeting to Black Twitter. I'm tweeting to feminist Twitter.' But a stranger in Australia or South America with a lot more followers can (and has) picked up tweets, reaching a whole new audience. The meaning becomes diluted or is taken out of context. And it can spiral from there.

With that in mind, what advice do I have to give?

Think before you tweet

Or snap, or stream, or whatever it is you post. This isn't about **not** posting something on social media – you shouldn't have to silence yourself to avoid negative attention. But pay some mind to what you want to say and whether you want to say it in that specific way at that specific time.

Inject some more realism and awareness into your online activity and behaviour. If you're posting publicly, anyone can see what you have to say – and even activities from private accounts can be screenshotted and shared. Take a few extra seconds of consideration before hitting send or publish. And take back the power by making a choice.

Think back to my story from earlier in the book, when my angry, spur-of-the-moment tweet after being accused of shoplifting led to me being in national newspapers and open to attacks. If I had stepped back and thought again, perhaps messaged my friends in a group chat instead, I could have avoided that path.

Be proactive, and think about the implications of your post. It isn't ideal, but we have to consider how we're going to come across — even if what we're saying should be uncontroversial.

A self-care fund

Before I get into this, I do want to address the fact that saving money for a rainy day **is** a privilege. I understand that not everyone reading this will be able to squirrel money away for the worst. Being able to step away from your online world and shut it out for a time is a luxury.

But if you have the capacity to do it, I recommend you try. You could open a new bank account — I have a special pot with Monzo as a break-in-case-of-emergencies solution. If you're out in town and that creepy stalker messages you again, you'll have some money to help you with private transportation to get you off the streets. If you need downtime and your house feels constricting, you can take yourself away somewhere for the weekend. It doesn't have to break the bank and you don't need to go so far as a trip. Sometimes treating myself to a box of Ferrero Rocher and a cold glass of Baileys is all the reset I need.

So, if you've been to a public event and you're feeling exhausted, why not get your favourite restaurant to deliver afterwards? You could use the fund to invest in a virtual assistant for a couple of hours to take the admin burden off your shoulders or even manage your social media posting so you can have a break. If you've been through a traumatic cycle of online abuse, you could look at a couple of weeks of therapy to talk through your situation.

You can also use this money to invest in solutions to directly deal with the abuse itself. A VPN, or software that helps you monitor certain online actions. For more serious offences, unfortunately, you might find yourself needing legal assistance, whether that's a simple legal letter or representation in court. Those are severe situations and will be mental battles in and of themselves, but having prepared for them financially will at least take some of the weight off your shoulders.

Tool 4: Curating your timeline

Something we often forget when existing online is that our social media accounts and online spaces are exactly that: they're *ours*. As such, it is well within your power to curate much healthier social media profiles. Ones that have only the content you want to see.

This step is about avoiding content you think could be harmful or triggering to you. You're under no obligation to allow strangers to run rampant in your online space, and you don't need a good reason to block them. It's time to unfollow all the social media accounts that don't work for you any more.

Reasons to follow and unfollow

This is something you can lay out in your page policy (see page 142), but it's worth diving into here. How will you define what constitutes behaviour worth unfollowing someone for? And what's the test to ensure they're someone worth following in the first place?

That's up to you and there are some points worth considering. I recommend looking through your follow lists on the social media platforms you use and asking yourself a few questions. First, is their content even relevant to you? If they aren't talking about your interests, don't engage with the communities you do or simply say nothing that interests you, consider unfollowing them. They might not be offensive, but they're also not adding anything to your online experience.

Next, ask if you find yourself complaining about their content more often than not. If you find yourself disagreeing with them

POSTING CONTENT DOESN'T MEAN THEY'RE CONTENT.

Create & Cultivate

regularly and often contemplate commenting and getting caught up in an argument, it's not worth your time or energy. And if they or by extension their posts make you angry or frustrated all the time, that's a definite unfollow. Create a relationship with social media that helps you recharge – not drains you.

Does their content align with your values? Sometimes you follow someone because they posted a funny meme once, or because you met them at a party that one time. But, eventually, you realize that their principles or stance on liberation are completely at odds with yours. Again, that constant conflict or the irritation you feel isn't worth it, and the likelihood is you'll never be able to change their mind with a couple of tweets.

Does following these accounts on your timeline make you feel inferior or like you're not enough? Does it even happen with people you admire? Remember, if you come away feeling worse about yourself, be self-compassionate and unfollow.

When you consider following someone new, ask yourself these same questions. Ultimately, you only want to be adding people who will be a positive influence on your online experience. You don't invite everyone you know or people you just met into your home, so you **don't** have to do so with your online space.

Changing your settings

There's more to curating your timeline. You can customize the experience even more with the settings on each social media platform. Unfortunately, without regulations in place, there's no standard set of features these platforms have to include, meaning how much you can insulate yourself from online abuse will vary. And with so many platforms available, it's impossible to list every setting you can change to stay safe.

But I'll run through some of the widely available settings I recommend changing. Though you might want to earmark some time to sit down and look at the settings of each of the platforms you use in more depth too. See what options are available to you; there'll no doubt be some you never even thought would be there.

A standard setting to change is who can and can't reply to you or your posts. It wasn't available then but there was a huge need for this option in 2020 following the murder of George Floyd. For the Black community, it was a highly stressful and emotional time, and what wasn't needed in the moment was for posts supporting Black Lives Matter to be overrun by trolls. Now on multiple platforms, you're able to restrict who can reply to your posts, setting it to only your followers and/or people you follow. It allows you to take control of the conversation in your own space. Now that you've curated the list of people you follow and audited those who follow you, you should be in a much safer position to engage with a values-aligned community. And if you want, you don't have to have replies at all. Shut off comments if you feel that's best.

You can also mute specific people or terms. Certain content can be triggering, such as the fallout of many Black Lives Matter protests or stories around #MeToo. Sometimes, you might just not want to engage with particular topics, such as the COVID-19 pandemic, because it adds too much negativity or anxiety to your life. By using the mute function, you can block out these conversations, even if it's just temporarily. This means you can be intentional about when you want to consume news and inform yourself about potentially triggering topics. If the news feeds your anxiety and makes you feel worse, mute it for a period of time.

Another feature to look into is turning off video autoplay. Twitter enables users to stop videos from playing as soon as you scroll to them. This means you don't have to see potentially triggering content, especially the kind sent by trolls to elicit a reaction.

Proactive blocking

A good habit to get into is pre-emptively blocking accounts that immediately scream 'problematic'. A scan of their recent tweets, their bio and use of certain emojis or flags gives a helpful indication. In the summer of 2020, a well-known celebrity was engaging in harmful behaviour online, predominantly towards Black women. I pre-emptively blocked them, giving me peace of mind. This meant I had the emotional capacity to support other Black women being harmed by this celebrity. They really should have been banned (and thankfully now have been), but in the meantime we can take those proactive steps to protect ourselves.

This is also good practice for troll accounts. You know the ones. They have the default Twitter or Instagram profile picture, they barely have any followers and their account was made very recently. The chances are, if these kinds of people are in your mentions causing you distress, they won't be open to changing their minds. It's best not to engage at all, and just block them before any damage can be done. There are also some helpful crowdsourced blocklists, as well as apps that allow you to share blocklists with friends. This can help starve the oxygen that trolls so greatly crave.

Some trolls are a little harder to spot, so it's worth learning to analyse when a person might not be arguing in good faith. Look at who they follow: if they don't follow anyone you know (or anyone at all), or predominantly follow nationalist, misogynistic or Islamophobic accounts, block! If their timeline is full of them trolling others, block!

If they do have a profile picture, use Google to do a reverse image search. This will show you if they stole it from somewhere else to hide who they really are. I did this around Christmas 2018, when an online stalker turned out to be using a lawyer's photo and name on Twitter. I found the real lawyer on Instagram, who was mortified and started legal action against the troll. On some platforms, you can also see if they've confirmed their email address; if they haven't, then block them.

This is without even touching on bots. Research shows this is where many of our online spaces are heading – or have already headed: bots being used to counter pro-social groups or campaigns. And I might sound like a conspiracy theorist, but there are plenty of state-bought bots.

Your online space is yours alone, and you're allowed to block, mute or filter out anyone or anything you want. This is the heart of digital self-care: looking after yourself. So don't let the trolls or negative people drag you down. All you should be concerned with is lifting yourself up.

Tool 5: Setting boundaries

How to create boundaries in our online space is such a valuable lesson. Consider your offline boundaries – would you accept someone constantly tapping you on the shoulder in person? Probably not. So why accept those constant nudges online?

A huge part of digital self-care is deciding what to be bothered by, and resisting the temptation to be bothered by everything. For most people, that's easier said than done. Some days you will feel strong enough, and others you won't. There's no playbook. There's no one way to deal with online abuse. You have to decide how you want to act.

Creating a page policy

Page policies are a great way to openly communicate your online boundaries and expectations, serving as an excellent method of digital self-defence. Your page policy might take the form of a pinned tweet, an email signature, Instagram highlight, a short post on your website, or any combination of these.

Aja Barber is someone with her own page policy: 'I try to put an arguments in my comments quickly. If it seems like it's getting

WHEN TWITTER BECAME AVAILABLE, I JOINED.
AND THEN INSTAGRAM ETC. BUT ALONG THE WAY,
SOCIAL MEDIA TURNED INTO A PLACE THAT
EXACERBATES THE WORST KIND OF

VITRIOL

TOWARDS HUMAN BEINGS,
OFTEN AND MOSTLY BLACK PEOPLE,
AND SPECIFICALLY BLACK WOMEN.
I AM CREATING NEW SOCIAL MEDIA RULES
AND GUIDELINES FOR MYSELF AND ALSO MY FOLLOWERS.
I WON'T BE RESPONDING TO OR ENGAGING WITH

TROLLS, REAL OR FAKE.

I WOULDN'T LET SOMEONE

YELL AND SCREAM

AT ME IN PERSON, SO WHY WOULD I

LET SOMEONE DO SO ONLINE?

I WON'T GIVE SOCIAL MEDIA MY WHOLE HEART AND SOUL. I AM NO LONGER
WILLING TO TREAT THE INTERNET LIKE GOD. IT'S ACTUALLY AND FACTUALLY

CREATED NEW TRAUMA FOR ME.

I WILL BE FOCUSING ON ABOLITION.

I WILL BE FOCUSING ON BLACK JOY, ART, AND CREATIVITY.
I WILL BE FOCUSING ON SHARING ABOUT THE WORK I'M DOING
THAT I CAN SPEAK AND ATTEST TO. AND LASTLY, SOCIAL MEDIA IS BUT
ONE TOOL TO USE TO GET US CLOSER TO FREEDOM. BUT THE WAY IT HAS BEEN

MANIPULATED AND CONTROLLED BY CAPITALISM

AND CORPORATIONS IS CREATING A NEW INFRASTRUCTURE

THAT DOESN'T VALUE HUMAN LIFE.

I CAN ATTEST TO THIS PERSONALLY.

Patrisse Cullors, Instagram, July 2019

petty, it's time to stop it. I don't let it bring down the mood of my post.' Aja shared with me how she sees engaging in these conflicts as being unsustainable: 'We're constantly thinking about now, now, now. But we've got to be thinking about the long term. And if I'm arguing with every asshat that wants to have an argument, I won't have the energy to do the work I want to do. There have been scenarios that have been so overwhelming that no one ends up doing the work that we're here for. And if that's the case, that's a loss for everyone.'

That's her philosophy, but consider what you want your own page policy to be. It should cover what you expect from those who engage in your online space. For example, it might include how you plan to respond (or not) to profanity, aggressive comments, misogyny, racism, sexism, ableism, homophobia and transphobia. It might also explain how you will engage with trolls, and indicate topics that aren't up for debate. It may also offer insight into the best channels to contact you through, or expected response times.

The goal of explaining these boundaries openly is that you no longer have to keep explaining yourself, or communicating with those who consistently overstep your boundaries.

So, let's go through creating one, step by step.

Step 1: Reflection

When creating your page policy, first take some time to pause and reflect. Think about what you're going to ask of other people, including friends, family, organizations and strangers you may encounter online. Decide how you're going to respond to any abuse and toxicity. What will you tolerate? Will you filter, mute and block? When will you engage? When will you expose? When will you ignore? When will you report? Who do you plan on reporting to?

It can feel overwhelming at first, because no one's ever asked you to do this. You've probably never even thought you **could** do this. But this is your online space – only you get to decide what that looks like for you.

Make a list of points that are important to you and where you think you might draw lines. Is your online space about joy and having fun? Do you have to use it for work as well? How will those coexist? Think about it for as long as you need. A lot of this will overlap with the intentions and values we discussed earlier on in this chapter.

Step 2: Criteria

Now we're looking at how people respond to you, and the messages they send. This step is about defining the criteria for you to take certain actions. For example, what constitutes a full block? Is there a level where you would engage with them? What would lead to a report? And to whom?

You get to define what is and isn't acceptable. If a gendered abusive word is enough to block someone, go for it. You don't have to engage with that. Start to lay out these criteria and form some basic rules.

An example of a list of criteria and rules might include:

1. No work or professional contact – send an email instead.
2. Abuse of any kind will be immediately blocked.
3. One re-explanation of boundaries, then you're out.
4. Don't engage with accounts who haven't verified their email address or phone number.

Step 3: Prepare your response

Outline what your response will be in relation to the criteria you set in step 2. I've found having a plan helps me minimize the emotional toll and the time. For example, I have a template response for those that solicit work through DMs, directing them to my website or work email. When I was a local politician I would be clear why I was blocking a resident and how else they could contact me if they needed my help. Your template response could start with, 'My identity is not up for debate', 'That's not an appropriate comment' or 'No'. Prepare to affirm your boundaries. If you see a comment or phrase you don't like and want to address it, what do you need to do to achieve this?

Your response might also be to put down your phone and not come back to the comment immediately – or at all. Or, thanks to your self-care fund, it might be to get away for a while.

Step 4: Seeking support

We've talked about the importance of community. Who will you lean on when you're in a storm of abuse or about to do a media engagement? Build up your support network now, and tell them about your policy. Let them into your thought process and show them what you'll need from them, such as emotional support or someone to help coordinate your digital self-care action plan for you.

This is the step where you'll want to define what else you want your family, friends, colleagues or employer to do. When I felt like I was in the spotlight and overexposed on both social and mainstream media, I asked friends and my colleagues on the local council to not share information about my location or post any personal images publicly until I felt safe again.

You may also want to ask a friend to help you moderate the abuse if you don't want to expose yourself to it. Make sure they know about online abuse and how it manifests. Chapter Seven of this book is a great starting point for allies.

Step 5: Communicate your policy

Now that you've done the internal work necessary to figure out who you want to be and how you want to exist online, it's time to consider sharing that with the world. If your page policy is a way to set out your online intentions and principles, as well as what you expect of others, you want to get it out there. Make it easily accessible to anyone who wants or needs it. Ultimately, this policy is for yourself, but it's helpful to communicate it proactively to others. Vicky Ford, MP for Chelmsford, has her page policy as a pinned post on her public Facebook page. I've seen others have their key boundaries in their bio: 'No DMs – for work requests, please email xxx@xxx.com'.

Remember, you set the limits for your online profiles, so let people know what you will and won't accept. Lay out your rules of engagement for your social media, and keep writing up any template response when you notice you're repeating yourself.

Trolls will do everything they can to get a rise out of you, but all you have to do is follow your policy. If they want to come into your mentions and behave like somebody with no manners, block them. Don't even think twice about it. You may also want to keep a copy of your policy on or near your computer and phone. This way, when trolls rear their ugly heads and emotions are high, you can simply refer to your policy, follow its guidance and move on. Worrying about them is not worth the energy, and you'll be surprised at just how much of a relief it is not to have to stress as much every time you face online abuse. Your resilience is like a muscle, and with practice it will get stronger.

A quick word on blocking

In the course of following through on your page policy, you're going to come across people you need to block, as is your right. There are people who will overstep your boundaries without a care in the world. You have the option to limit what they see, mute them or indeed block them entirely.

And you should never feel guilty for it. In 2019, Labour MP Diane Abbott blocked a well-known antagonistic right-wing journalist. She sent a strong signal that politicians, particularly women, can curate a safer online space. They don't have to engage with someone they don't want to, even if they are an elected official. After all, mockery, abuse and harassment are not forms of democratic engagement, nor legitimate ways to hold politicians to account.

You don't have to give a reason every time you block someone, but it can be good to re-communicate your boundaries publicly to your other followers. There are a few stock phrases you can use, either before blocking someone or to let them (and others) know they've violated your boundaries:

> *'I would prefer not to discuss that.'*
> *'I don't have the capacity for this conversation right now.'*
> *'Thank you for sharing.'*
> *'That's not your business.'*
> *'I'm uncomfortable with the way you're speaking to me.'*
> *'I haven't formed an opinion on that yet and would prefer not to be pressured into making one.'*

Think of the block and report functions on social media as your armour, plus the mute and filter options on Twitter. It's also good practice in enforcing your own page policy – it's only as good as your commitment to it!

Of course, this is a two-way street: you might be the one being blocked. You don't have the right not to be blocked. And that's fine. Whether for fair or unfair reasons, you can't demand someone interact with you. You wouldn't want that from someone you blocked. Just something to keep in mind.

Tools to help you enforce your boundaries

Blocking is just one of the tools available to you. While tech companies can (and should) do more, there are other options on various social media platforms that you can use to customize your experience.

Maryam Hasnaa has her own rules of engagement online. She is immersed in the world of mysticism and spirituality, and teaches people how to live out their true purpose. She talks often about the boundaries she's set: 'This might not be for everyone, but my mentions have been on mute for over two years now. If I choose to engage with people online, it's all up to me. You can customize all areas of your life for what works best for your well-being. Unapologetically.'

That's just one option you can choose. Other tools for dealing with online abuse might include:

- Deleting your social media account or making it private
- Amending notification settings
- Having a phone ban during certain hours
- Removing read receipts
- Turning off your 'last online' information
- Muting, restricting or blocking certain people, words or hashtags
- Having a friend read comments for you
- Turning off comment functionality
- Restricting who can reply to your tweets

Tool 6: Time management

Our brains aren't equipped to handle a constant stream of notifications, emails, Netflix binging and twenty-four-hour news. Especially not on top of an already-hectic forty-hour work week and packed social life. But it feels like today we're always 'on'. There's always a screen in front of us – and even when we're asleep, it's right by our side. There aren't enough hours in the day for us to dedicate so much time to our devices, and sometimes what we need is to switch off. Let our minds go quiet and rest.

I know what it's like to feel like you need to be attached to your accounts 24/7. That if you take your eye off them for one second, you'll miss out on the most important story ever. And when you're facing online abuse, it can be tempting to go back and fight your corner, or read one more terrible message. But you can leave. You can step back. For yourself, for your family and for your friends. The most crucial part of your digital self-care toolkit is the ability to do that and say no. To make the choice to walk away when the situation gets too much for you. If you're constantly in fight mode, you have no time to heal.

Adam Wagner has a brilliant analogy regarding the online space and his participation in it. He looks at it as if he is a video game character, with his own energy bar. Every time he enters a situation that leads to abuse, a personal attack or general hostility, it eats away at his energy. So, before entering what could be considered the danger zone, he takes a beat to think, 'Am I going to do that thing I know is going to deplete my energy bar? How much energy will I have left?'

Speaking about this philosophy, he told me: 'As important as an issue might be to me personally, it might not be worth getting involved in certain situations. I've got to make quite hard decisions about engaging because I only have a finite amount of energy. If I get to the bottom of that bar – and I have several times – the people that suffer are the people around me. That might be my family or my friends. And they know because I take it out on them. My wife always knows when I'm arguing on Twitter because I'm distracted, and hostility comes out in my everyday life. Who needs that? I was feeling exhausted by interacting with the platform, and I realized it's not worth it.'

We aren't machines – we're only human – and this belief that you need to be switched on constantly is only hurting you. Your well-being is a finite resource. It's up to you to choose where your energy is spent.

So, what little rules can you introduce into your life to help you manage your time online?

Take regular breaks

It's healthy to take breaks so you can let your energy bar fill back up. You need to give yourself that mental space to recover. The best way to make sure you do this is to make it a regular habit.

To start, look at how much time you spend online. You can do a rough estimate, or check the screen time statistics on your phone. There are also some great apps for this. These should tell you how many hours you spend using apps such as your web browser or social media platforms. Having that number in front of you will help you realize just how much time you're dedicating to something that isn't necessarily helping you.

Then commit to a time during the day where you have no tech. I try to do this most mornings and keep the beginning of the day to myself. Block off an hour for yourself: read a book, take a bath or even do absolutely nothing. When I treat myself to a manicure, I keep my phone in my pocket and make the most of someone else keeping my hands busy.

It could be anything that gets you away from your screen. Think of it like a digital less-sugar option, and cut out the screen time.

The more you practise this, the easier it will be and ultimately the healthier your relationship with tech will be.

Manage your notifications

Something you can do is to pay attention to what notifications you get during a particular day. When we're not attuned to it, we don't realize just how many flood our senses. The odds are that almost every app on your phone is capable of sending you notifications.

Look at your phone's settings and see which apps have permission to send notifications. Decide which ones should lose their privileges. You don't have to commit to this permanently; you can always change them back if you decide you want to.

Many phones will also have an option to set a quiet period where you don't receive any notifications. This is great when used in tandem with your breaks from social media.

Walking away

Never argue with an idiot. They will drag you down to their level and beat you with their experience.

   Mark Twain

One of the key messages that stuck with me throughout all of the conversations featured in this book is that our lives aren't social media. Yes, they're becoming increasingly intertwined, but we need to realize that we can also find escapism outside of the online space.

We don't work every hour of every day, we only sleep for so long, and it's even recommended to have rest days away from the gym. As the saying goes, too much of a good thing can eventually be bad for you. But when it comes to the internet, we can't seem to drop it. How many of us look at our phones just before we go to sleep, and then right as we wake up? I know I'm guilty of this.

If you need a time-out or a break, then take one. Especially if you're currently suffering from abuse first-hand. This is where a digital self-care routine comes into play. Our bodies and minds need rest.

There can be this false and unhelpful narrative that if you're not always switched on and fighting your trolls, you can't be all that bothered about the abuse. That you can't be a real feminist if you're not fighting the cause every minute you're awake. That you're not a true activist if you're not standing up to people rather than silently muting, blocking, trimming and removing. This mentality isn't working for anyone. It's not sustainable. We're not helping the causes we care about or the movements we support by burning ourselves out. The perception that being busy equals greater success or productivity is flawed and outdated. It's a capitalist notion of labour that's been brought into liberation movements. But that's not how activism works. The urgency is unhelpful and, frankly, unhealthy for any cause. Audre Lorde famously said it herself: 'Caring for myself is not self-indulgence, it is self-preservation, and that is an act of political warfare.' So give yourself that space.

It's similar to Gabby Jahanshahi-Edlin. She's not on Twitter – I'd love it if she was – but that's her way of taking charge of her digital self-care and I love that more! She uses Facebook to talk to only one person. She'll log into Instagram once a day for five minutes to look at a couple of posts and then she'll delete the entire app again. That's her chosen relationship with the online world.

She told me: 'There are parts of being online that I love. But the downsides are too big for me now. It's not the trolling or even people commenting asking silly questions about antisemitism. It's that I don't want to live there. But there is of course a sense of FOMO. "I'm not going to know what's going on." It's either I know everything that's going on all the time and I'm stressed all the time, or I live life a bit more gently.' Something Gabby mentioned in our conversation is the 'privilege to step away'. She acknowledges that she's in a fortunate position to be able to step away for good. But for others, that's not possible.

As we discussed in an earlier chapter, some rely on the online space for community and support. It's their outlet for finding people who understand them. By taking that away, they're removing their access to that self-curated help. Then there are those who rely on the online space for their livelihood. More than two billion people worldwide purchased goods online in 2020. Just think how much competition there is, all vying for this attention. An online business using social platforms is like a digital shopfront, and the internet is the high street. Offline, a shopfront is how you draw people in. If it's vandalized, it's considered a crime. If someone spray-paints over the front or smashes the windows, we as a society know that's wrong. But online, where so many people – including marginalized people – make a living, we don't treat their digital storefronts the same. And, as discussed earlier, they can end up facing significant financial and emotional harm as a result. But they can't always afford to walk away entirely. Which is why digital self-care is sometimes about taking a step back temporarily so that you're able to return stronger at a later date.

Taking control

Receiving online abuse – no matter what form – is traumatic, and it transports you into a state of hypervigilance. It's important to take the time to wind down from this heightened mental chaos. What small steps can you take?

As early as is appropriate for you following abuse, do something that helps you find peace again. This could be yoga, stretching, getting outside, doing arts and crafts to keep your hands busy, reading a book, going to your favourite park or restaurant or calling a friend.

Why not take some time now to make a list of all your favourite activities and who you enjoy doing them with? Are there friends who instantly brighten your day? Or do you prefer solo activities? Where is your favourite place to find zen? What form of exercise do you most enjoy? Then, whenever you feel you need to escape – if only for five minutes – you can refer to your list and find a way to reset your mind.

Tool 7: Community

Critical to keeping yourself on track and accountable in terms of your online presence and safety is building a supportive, uplifting community of people to share your journey with. This is otherwise known as 'collective digital self-care'.

If you're entering the public domain with an increased risk of

YOU ARE
NOT OBLIGATED
TO REMAIN IN
ANY ENVIRONMENT
THAT CONTINUALLY
DEPLETES YOU
AND DOES NOT
NOURISH YOU.

Lalah Delia, Instagram, September 2021

online abuse or are actively under fire from someone, you're effectively going into battle. And it's always better to have people by your side.

It's imperative that you have a network of people you can go to, even if you're fortunate enough never to experience abuse first-hand. It's always better to pre-empt the occurrence of abuse and have a circle of people you know you can trust and who will understand.

Building this community for yourself is about identifying the people you want to learn alongside and grow with. It might be loved ones from your offline life, or anyone you've met in online communities who share your intentions and values, or a combination of any other online or offline acquaintances. They should be supportive individuals you *want* to surround yourself with – both while things are good and you're thriving online, and if things turn sour and you need direct support and guidance. This community should be a safe space in which you can share tips, as well as acting as a support network as and when you need it. It might be who you go to when you want to be consoled after receiving abuse, to hold you accountable in keeping to your online values and principles, or for backup when you're taking some much-needed time out.

Once you identify who these people are, sit down with them (metaphorically or literally) and talk about what you do and don't want for your online life. Share with them your page policy. Communicate your intentions and expectations, and ask them to hold you accountable.

Identify how you'll show up for each other both on- and offline. Share how you want to deal with abuse should it happen, and how they can support you to do so. What they should remind you of if you're ever in the depths of despair, or how they can lift you out of the slump. Gather the same information from them. Have an open, transparent dialogue about what victim blaming means to you and how you can avoid it. Discuss how you plan to use any privilege you might have online and how you can be an ally for others. Be open and honest about how you can hold space for one another.

Even if you don't yet have a predefined support community, I still implore you to share your page policy and online intentions with others. That might be with a friend, parent or partner. Anyone in your life you trust and know you can count on. You want those around you to know if you'd rather they avoid engaging with trolls on your behalf and stoking the fire. Communicate with them so they know how to show up for you without inadvertently victim blaming or accidentally perpetuating harm.

Refuse to suffer in silence

One of the most important self-care tips: **don't suffer in silence**.

Online abuse is a serious concern, and you're not burdening anyone by sharing your experience. Even if it's been a few weeks or months now, and you feel you shouldn't still be bothered. Talk to your community about what's happening and how it makes you feel. Ask them to actively listen and to validate you. You can ask for help to document and report the abuse if you've decided this is the course of action you want to take. Seek support from loved ones if deciding to make a report to the relevant authority.

Conversations with others help us to mould the future. What worked and didn't work in a situation? What can we learn from each other? How can we better prepare? Healthy conversations lead to growth and collective liberation. When we're not actively inviting such conversations, we can't learn from one another. We're not building our toolkit, we're not learning for next time and, worse, we're not equipping future generations for a beast that's only going to grow.

Laura Bates is a big advocate for leaning on her support structure: 'When it comes to my own personal digital self-care, I found using an external team a big help. If I asked a family member to filter my communications, because of the death and rape threats, it would be incredibly painful for them to read them too. When I launched my book *Men Who Hate Women*, we knew we were poking a hornets' nest and anticipated a backlash. So my publishers hired a digital security expert to monitor where the book was being mentioned and what was being said. Other people can be part of our toolkit and digital self-care without having to be inside our inner circle.

'The only thing that I found has worked has been having a network and communication with other women in the same situation, because nobody else gets it. Even friends and family who are so loving and kind and caring haven't experienced it. And I remember I was talking to [feminist writer] Clementine Ford about my experience and felt this rush of relief. I realized it was because she was one of the only people in the whole world who had exactly the same specific experiences.'

Speak to the right people

Often, that first conversation after being subjected to online abuse will be the hardest to initiate. Even if you've got an extensive online community of allies, when you're in the moment, it can feel as if you're in a royal rumble with everyone else versus you.

When I told my Nigerian mother about my abuse, she didn't understand. She grew up in a different generation. And when I told the police and the council I was representing, they didn't know what to do or say. When I told my boyfriend on our date, however, we sat down and spoke openly about how he could hold space for me and he asked what I needed from him.

A lot of people suffer in silence and, sadly, that's what the trolls want. They want you to feel isolated and all alone. To think you deserve their abuse. Then you sit in silence so long that you end up staying quiet out of fear that no one will understand.

This is why selecting the right person or people to share your experience with is key. Think about the different areas of your life. Who could you speak to in your family? Who out of your friends is best to talk to? What about in your professional life? Who in your digital self-defence community is your first port of call? If you're in the public eye it's also worth having a contingency plan with your agent.

You don't want to wait until you're already struggling and suffering to identify who these people are for you. By building your community and support network now, you can more easily transition into healing mode should you experience abuse in the future. And this isn't just a community for you; it's a community for everyone. They'll be there when you need them, but you also have to show up for them when they need it too. You're a part of **their** community, after all – and there's strength in numbers.

Tool 8: Aftermath and trauma

Unfortunately, abuse doesn't end when you click out of a disgusting comment or email. It doesn't end with you blocking the account or reporting the message. It's pervasive and persistent. And even if you follow the tips so far, it doesn't mean you'll escape unscathed. This part of the digital self-care toolkit is about looking after yourself in the aftermath.

Trauma left unchecked can snowball into something much worse. So for the benefit of your well-being, it's worth being introspective and working out the ways that you need soothing. My tell-tale signs are flashbacks, overwhelming emotions or recurring memories. It might also involve nightmares, or flinching at the slightest noise.

Recovery is not linear – nor is it an excuse for abusing others. Unmanaged emotional control or anger issues aren't healthy for anyone. So how can you take steps towards healing?

Holding exercise

Psychologist Dr Peter Levine – who was a stress consultant with NASA and is a renowned expert in stress and trauma – has a self-holding exercise I find useful. PTSD and trauma can leave you feeling overwhelmingly scattered in the moment. 'Self-holding' helps to reverse this fractured feeling with a self-hug, to show ourselves and our mind that we aren't broken – that we're contained. This exercise can bring you back to a state of calm.

The following is a five-step version of the self-holding exercise that I came across in my Instagram explore page:

1. Place your hands on either side of your head, and hold for a few moments.
2. Place one hand on your forehead and one hand on the back of your head, breathing through the hold.
3. Move your hand from the back of your head to your heart, still holding your forehead.
4. Keep your hand on your heart, moving the other down to your stomach, maintaining a firm pressure and calm breathing throughout.
5. Finally, keeping your hand on your stomach, move your other hand to the base of your head, to the deepest indent above the nape of your neck.

You can do this lying down, sitting at your desk, eyes open, eyes closed – whatever works for you. The idea is to bring yourself back to a state of presence and calm.

Checking attachment styles after trauma

Attachment styles are something we apply to relationships. The idea is that every adult has one of the four main attachment styles: secure, anxious, avoidant and fearful-avoidant. We use this categorization to explain why people behave the way they do in relationships, but I find it can also be applied to how we cope with trauma and abuse.

me, I was an anxious type when it came to online abuse. I keep running back to the comments to see what had been said. I put this weight on my shoulders that I had to try to save everyone from online abuse, but that's just not possible. That anxious attachment style drove me to burnout.

It's important that we acknowledge how we naturally respond to online abuse. What is our first instinct? Put words to your feelings, and see what the common thread is. Look up the 'feelings wheel' – a visual breakdown of all kinds of specific emotions. Studies show that if you can adequately describe an emotion, your brain is more able to process it. So not just 'joy' or 'anger', but something more specific – for instance, 'hopefulness' or 'frustration'. This should let you hone in on what you feel in your trauma and help you identify your triggers.

Transformative resilience

So far, digital self-care has been about looking after yourself. A great word to describe this aspect is 'resilience'. You have to be resilient to attacks and have the strength to bounce back, recognizing the activities you can do and the actions you can take to encourage this. It's something I talked about with author Ama Marston, who discussed the term 'transformative resilience', which she introduced in her work.

'You often hear about this notion of resilience as bouncing back,' she said. 'And this is a narrative that originally comes from metallurgy and the idea of bending metal and seeing if it can go back to its original form. So it wasn't even originally about humans. I co-authored a book with my mother, who's a psychologist, and together we noticed through our individual and professional experiences – as well as research across disciplines – that we don't often bounce back.

'Transformative resilience is the ability or the process of using challenges and stresses as a catalyst for growth and innovation. It's about forward motion – what we can learn, the strengths we can build from difficult experiences, and the new ways of operating in the world that can come from it. And that can be true for an individual, a leader, a whole organization or a community.

'But again, it's looking at a kind of evolution and how we use challenging experiences to propel ourselves forward. And a key part of that is acknowledging losses, difficulties and disappointments, and making sure we veer away from a kind of toxic positivity.'

That last point is so important to consider. There's a trend for self-love and loving every part of you. Taken to the extreme, it's the idea that you can do no wrong. But the cycle of toxic positivity is just as much of a trap as self-criticism and negative thinking. By only looking on the bright side of life, you wilfully ignore the darker parts. In all my advice so far, it's about facing up to what's in front of you. Digital self-care isn't about ignoring the hate that comes your way, because you can never do that. And if you say you can, you're kidding yourself. You're just shoving it in the closet and pretending it doesn't exist. It's not the way. Self-love is important, but it can't replace self-care. Strength and honesty aren't the easiest things to sell on Instagram, but they're absolutely vital.

As Ama explained, we can only grow by acknowledging the harder parts of our lives: 'We need to have faith that we have the resources to get through trauma, take care of ourselves, and learn from it. And if we don't have the resources ourselves, we know that we are able to leverage the support of others, including professionals, to help us heal and grow. At the time we're under attack, that is not likely to be the time we're going to be able to make a change or draw the initial lessons. Eventually, you get a little distance from it. And you start to have an "a-ha moment". That's the catalyst for change.'

So, in the online world, when you receive that disrupting comment that throws you into chaos, you have to withdraw to protect yourself. As I said earlier, it's okay to detach from online platforms. Then, in time, that light-bulb moment will come. Your approach will change. You might start to experiment with how much you engage and where you engage. This is you gaining some distance from a difficult experience, and integrating the lessons you learn from it into a new normal. It's an iterative process.

You can't be an agent of change if you're not coming from a place of health. You have to have agency over your well-being, mindset, skills and behaviour. You growing and evolving in the face of abuse is you saying you don't accept the status quo. You don't accept all the messages you get. You don't accept being shoehorned into a victim mentality. As humans, we have this amazing capacity for growth. It might be our greatest feature. But as we get older, it takes more effort to learn.

There's a misconception that healing will happen quickly. But that in itself can be trauma-inducing. If you're still in the midst of pain or difficulty and you or someone you know is trying to rush you into finding the lessons, it's not going to work. You have to come to these moments by yourself. There's a reason Ama called it an 'a-ha moment' – it comes when it comes.

Steps to healing

When it comes to healing from online abuse, the first few moments and days can be critical. You're stuck in your body's stress response, firing on all cylinders, unsure which way to turn. Mamta Saha told me about the five steps of self-care that she always advocates using in those moments:

1. *Mind* – What are you telling yourself? Is it true or false?
2. *Body* – What is your body language? Are you loose or tense? Are you clenched or free?
3. *Heart* – Are you grounded in the moment? What is your intuition telling you? And what are you telling yourself?
4. *Breath* – Is it shallow? Is it deep? Are you even breathing at all?
5. *Truth* – What is the fundamental truth of the situation? As in, what is **your** truth?

By working through these five steps, you can push past the initial emotions and get out of your fight-freeze-flight response. It's a way of recentring yourself in your surroundings, and noticing what happens to your mind and body when you experience digital abuse.

Let's look at this process in action in a hypothetical scenario. You've got another message in your DMs. It's somebody calling you a slut because you posted a picture of yourself wearing a short skirt. Now, you can let it eat away at you, making you furious or self-conscious. Or you can take a moment.

Step one, **mind**. What are you telling yourself? Do you agree with the comment? Do you honestly think you're a slut? Then ask if that's objectively true. Of course it isn't – it was a picture.

Then the **body**. How does your body feel? Are your shoulders hunched? Are you curling up inside yourself? It's what we do when we feel insecure and self-conscious. Unclench. Let yourself feel loose. You'll notice how it makes you feel better.

Next is the **heart**. What is your intuition saying to you? Deep down, do you know that the photo was actually pretty great? That you look fantastic? That's why you uploaded it in the first place.

Now, your **breath**. In Mamta's words, your breathing is very telling. It's your life force energy. Are you filled up with that life force energy, or has it been sucked out? When we experience trauma, our breathing becomes shallow and short, and in times of panic we veer on the side of hyperventilation. Reset your breath to feel calmer. Deep breaths have a relaxing effect on the body. Slowly inhale, hold for a beat, and then exhale. Try counting to ten very slowly, while taking deep breaths.

Finally, **truth**. Not generic truth – but **your** truth. That is, you're a good person and you don't deserve this. Something's not right here and you need to do something about it.

By following these steps, you can pull yourself out of that perpetual cycle of feeling under threat. You can move to a place where you're able to be proactive and move forward, rather than only being reactive.

Your complete digital self-care toolkit

Those are my essential pieces of advice for navigating the World Wide Web. The tools for digital self-care are already in your toolkit – you just need to know how to access them. When we're lost in a sea of abuse and harassment online, it can feel impossible to crawl out of it. When it becomes your whole world, where's the escape? It's in you. Your head. Your heart. You know how to escape. You know how to walk away and do that digital detox.

Should you have to? No. In an ideal world, the internet would be free of the kind of vitriol that seeks to drive you away. But that sadly isn't the case. In lieu of help from anyone else, these tips are what you can do to support yourself. If you can master this mindset, you can grow into something so much stronger.

Chapter Six: Stepping up your digital security and self-defence

What do you do when you leave the house? You lock your doors, right? And when you're in a car, you put your seat belt on. If you ride a bike, you put a helmet on. We take steps like these to keep ourselves safe offline.

Even online, we take some precautions. We have antivirus software to protect us from viruses. We use strong passwords to stop our accounts being hacked. But how should we take our well-being and safety online more seriously, and utilize the ways to up our digital self-defence?

The presence of online abuse doesn't have to prevent you from sharing your views, connecting with others or taking the next step forward in your career. If anything, self-censorship and avoidance tactics only harm victims further, while simultaneously never getting to the root of the issue.

With the right and consistent approach, we can begin to take back control of our online presence and the access others have to us. We can be more considerate and thoughtful about what we're sharing, where we're sharing it and who we share it with. And we can put in place simple levels of protection to minimize our risk. It's about forming new habits to increase our digital security and bolster our line of defence against online threats. Taking that first step in building any new habit is often difficult, but it's only by taking it that we can begin to build the defence muscle we need to continue developing. We identified the potential dangers and harms in earlier chapters, and it's now about countering them, strategizing both individually and with our community, and mitigating their impact.

We're all still frustratingly waiting for tech companies and governments to join the party and do their part. So, in the meantime, it's about controlling what we can right now. About protecting ourselves and our right to exist and engage online. I know you might have heard this all before, and some of you are probably rolling your eyes. I get it. I once rolled my eyes and batted away the importance of digital security too. That was, until I faced various forms of online abuse and began noticing the different tactics and joining the dots.

Still, the notions of online security and protection aren't exactly the sexiest of topics. Setting different passwords for every online account? Yawn. I used to believe that kind of thing wasn't practical or realistic. But after the video of me first went viral, and a few months before the racist abuse began, I was hacked. And it made me realize how critical it is to invest regular time and energy into digital security.

Digital security is digital self-defence

Online self-defence is doing whatever is within your power to protect yourself. It's not too dissimilar from offline self-defence, such as taking a martial arts class. Consider all the potential risks online, and do what you can to minimize the likelihood of them happening to you – or the impact they're able to have on you and your mental health if they do. Not only is this important for yourself, it's also vital for your loved ones.

Psychologist Mamta Saha agrees that digital security is a necessary extension of our digital self-care toolkit. One of the key ways she suggests victims respond to abuse in the moment is by taking stock of their digital security: 'If they were on the receiving end of [abuse], I would ask them to have a look at any vulnerable aspect of their life that may be threatened, and identify what they can do to tighten up their security and privacy. That's the first thing: let's look at if there are any holes and, if there are, let's create some safety around those things, changing passwords, etc.'

You should see digital self-defence as not only being fully aware of risks and putting controls in place to protect yourself in the first place, but also as your first defence if a situation should arise. As Mamta says, check for any gaps and vulnerabilities before you turn your attention to healing. I speak from personal experience when I say that my unpreparedness and a feeling of defencelessness contributed massively to the pain of my abuse.

We have the knowledge to change our behaviour and adjust our way of thinking when online. Now we need to equip ourselves with the tools.

Perform an online audit

While online abuse shouldn't be a deterrent to being where you want to be, it is useful to consider if you really want to be in certain spaces or not. How many of us have old accounts from our younger years we no longer use? Or have an account on a certain platform because everyone else does, despite the fact it makes us feel shitty to engage with it?

I'll let you in on a secret: you don't have to be on every single platform. If you're not using one of your accounts, what harm will come from taking it down? If you do plan to stay on certain platforms, despite not using them, at the very least consider the personal data that's stored on them for everyone to see.

I recommend you take the time to perform an online audit for yourself. It's a great way to reduce your risks and vulnerabilities. Take stock of where you are – both old and current accounts. Familiarize yourself with every account you have, taking the time to figure out if each one is something you want to keep or are best deleting.

Assess them according to your newly defined online intentions and objectives. Do they align? Is your Twitter upholding the code of conduct you've set for yourself? Does your Instagram feed respect the boundaries of privacy you've now committed to? Even if you scroll all the way back to when you first got the account?

The end goal is to have a handful of live accounts that you regularly use and that serve a positive purpose in your life – be that sparking joy, engaging in healthy debate, for work, or keeping in touch with friends. And all of these accounts should uphold your intentions and boundaries. It takes time to scroll through years' worth of posts and pictures, but it's worth it to take back ownership of your online presence and reduce your chances of harm.

Let's dive deeper. Here are some questions you can ask yourself while auditing your online persona. They'll provide some food for thought, and help you perform a more thorough cleanse of your accounts.

Where can you protect yourself?

It's all too easy to set up accounts and forget about them. I'd bet plenty of us have a large online footprint, despite only being active in a small section of it. When looking at your online presence, it's important to first consider all the places people could have access to you. See if any of these match any profiles you have:

- Blogs or long-form content you've written
- Recorded events, in person or online
- Social media apps, such as Facebook or Twitter
- Work social media and communication platforms, such as LinkedIn, Slack, Asana and Trello
- Messaging apps, such as WhatsApp or Telegraph
- Video or image apps, such as YouTube, TikTok and Snapchat
- Chat rooms and forums

If you're a business owner, it's worth adding another layer of protection, especially if you work from home. Companies House and business directories like Yell display your personal details publicly. If you've worked as a non-executive director or a charity trustee, your details could be listed with the Charity Commission and on the charity's website. Luckily, it's quite easy to set up a virtual address online, or most accountants are happy to let you use theirs.

What can you protect against?

When it comes to cleansing your online accounts, there are a number of avenues to take. It will help to go through in a logical order:

1. Review your accounts

To start, you want to look at any accounts you might have abandoned. It might be worth pulling any personal data off them and deleting them entirely. If you don't use an old Facebook account and it houses your whole evolution from twelve years old, exposing all the thoughts and feelings you had while you were still figuring out who you are, is it worth keeping that information about you out there?

2. Review text

The first content to look at should be anything you've written, such as social media posts or blogs. Especially if you've had the same account since you were a teenager. Look for the writing that no longer aligns with your morals and values today. On social media, this could be anything you said in anger and posted on the spur of the moment. Or it could be a controversial blog that you no longer stand by. Anything that could be used against you, especially if it doesn't reflect who you are today. If so, deleting it might be a good idea. While it won't eliminate screenshots people could have taken in the past, it does prevent anyone else from taking any new ones.

This isn't about avoiding accountability, but rather modelling your online presence after the person you currently are.

There are a number of apps that allow people to delete social media posts at regular intervals. Glitch shares this as a tool in our digital self-care and defence training for women and non-binary people in public life, and as part of our digital citizenship education for young people in schools.

3. Review images and videos

The same goes for any images and videos that could damage your reputation if taken out of context. You know the ones – that girls' trip to Magaluf in 2013. Look through all your photo albums online, and ask yourself if you're comfortable keeping these images displayed or not. Even if you don't end up deleting them, it's worth it to at least give them a second glance and make peace with the possible repercussions ahead of time.

4. Review future posts

When it comes to future posts, why not create your own privacy checklist in your head? Set personal guidelines that force you to ask if the content you want to post contains private information that you don't want to expose. Remember that you aren't just sharing it with your followers. Other people may stumble across it in time. So make sure you're 100 per cent comfortable putting it out there. You don't have to mute and censor yourself; you're simply assessing what you're comfortable sharing, and making more informed decisions.

Another factor you can consider is how much you want to be seen. There's nothing wrong with being controversial, but a public profile means anyone and everyone can see your content, and perpetrators of abuse will often see this as you inviting conflict into your space. Are you comfortable with that? Or would you rather build a private community full of like-minded people and grow your online space that way?

Who might you need to protect against?

Next, it's worth taking a look at who you're connected with. A common belief is that online abuse comes from anonymous users. And while this is the case for a large proportion of online abuse, it's sadly not always the case. In Glitch's *Ripple Effect* report, the majority of online abuse reported by respondents was perpetrated by strangers – accounts or people that they did not know prior to the incident. However, 16 per cent experienced online abuse from acquaintances, 11 per cent from a partner or ex-partner, and 9 per cent from a colleague or superior at work.

Sometimes it can be an acquaintance who has become close to you purely for the purpose of inflicting abuse in the future. Or it might be an ex who starts harassing you when you've called the relationship off. Perhaps using images you've sent them against you, maybe in exchange for money. It could be a colleague from work with whom you've never quite seen eye to eye. When I spoke with Adam Wagner, he talked about how he was the victim of horrific antisemitic abuse for years. And all along, the perpetrator was another lawyer from his workplace.

This isn't intended to scare you into being distrustful of everyone around you, but rather to push you into evaluating your network and any risks they might pose.

Think of all the people you're connected with and evaluate their access to you. If your intuition is telling you something feels off with a certain digital connection, honour that and try restricting their access for a while. Anyone who openly shows distaste towards people based on their gender, sexual orientation, ethnic or religious background, disability or anything else is someone you should consider most in your evaluation.

At the very least, it's worth segmenting your followers/friends in order to restrict who has access to certain types of posts. For example, you might have a close-knit circle of contacts who are free to see and engage with anything you post, and a list who only get the abridged version of your digital content. I'm an avid user of the Close Friends feature on Instagram; for me this is a group of friends I trust with my personal content.

Another step might be to consider all the forms of abuse we discussed in Chapter Three and reverse-engineer them to minimize your own risk of becoming a victim. For example, sextortion relies on someone having explicit content of you in the first place. It's absolutely your right to share your body however you please, and in no way your fault if someone abuses your trust. But some extra caution about how you're sharing such content, and who with, can significantly help to reduce your risk of harm.

Stalking relies on a person knowing where you are and being able to track your movements. If this is something that concerns you, you can turn your location settings off, not post the businesses that you frequent and make it harder for people to guess where you are. Or, if you're posting in easily recognizable locations, you can skew the timeline. If you have friends who are open about their location and always tag you in posts, be sure to speak with them to ensure they avoid tagging you.

Once you know the where, what and who, you can regularly audit and edit your online presence to better serve you. Because your online life is exactly that: **yours**. Whether you're purposely in the public domain, want to keep your content private or are an active online ally for others, regularly checking in with your accounts and gauging your risk allows you to keep yourself as safe as possible.

Pre-emptive checklist

Now we've gathered this information from our audit, it's time to think about the steps we can take to keep ourselves safe in the future. After all, being online is a bit of a minefield. There's so much you need to avoid, and I wouldn't blame you if you find it overwhelming. I always try to draw lessons from others to help me protect myself.

I spoke with Laura Bates about how she keeps herself safer online, and it was an insightful and educational conversation. She said: 'I find that prevention is much better than response. It's much easier than trying to deal with abuse afterwards. For me, it's about taking every possible bit of personal information offline. It's a sacrifice, but I don't share any personal images or information about myself and my family, including my address, phone number and location.

'If I'm interviewed, I ask to have the photos taken somewhere away from my home and I ask interviewers not to mention where they've come to meet me. I regularly use tools to do searches on myself, to check that information hasn't somehow been leaked or popped up anywhere, and if it has, I request that information be taken down and then will go back and double-check that it's happened. I lock down privacy settings on my social media pages and have completely different, complicated passwords for every platform. It's time-consuming and difficult, but it means that if someone is attempting to hack you, they don't have access to everything.

'I went through a phase where people would regularly try to hack into the Everyday Sexism Twitter account. I'd receive a flurry of warning messages and time-out reminders, so two-step verification stopped that. Buying privacy services for any domains you register for work helps add a layer of protection too.'

Like Laura says, it sounds time-consuming and difficult, but being safe is about being proactive. You can be as cautious as humanly possible and *still* find yourself at risk of online abuse or harm. It's relentless, I know. But it is worth putting that extra, pre-emptive layer of digital security in place sooner rather than later.

Before you do, there are a few tips I want to pass on that are well worth running through.

Passphrases instead of passwords

The obvious one is to set strong passwords. Having your password as '1234' isn't going to cut it, I'm afraid. Similarly, if your birthday and memorable dates are easily accessible on your profiles, and you've also set these as your passwords, you're effectively giving someone the keys to your online space. You want to create a unique, complex password for each account you have. And keep changing them regularly; we've been told to change our passwords since the release of Windows 97, yet many of us still don't.

You should also enable two-factor authentication for all your personal and professional accounts. Each time you log in, you'll need a code (sent to you as a text/phone call or via an app), making the log-in process doubly secure.

When it comes to all these steps, while they can be a pain in the ass, they're essential. See it as double-locking your front door. If you find it a faff getting into your accounts, so will those who are trying to hack you. And we don't want to wait until we've already been hacked to put these protections in place. I know it's worth it because – as I said earlier – I've lived it.

Of course, it's difficult remembering all the passwords that are going to keep you safe, so it's worth investing in password management software to keep your details secure. Then you can avoid having them where people can find them, like a Post-it note on your desk or the notes app on your phone.

Separate your work and personal accounts

If possible, keep separate work and personal accounts to minimize the chance that people in your professional network are able to reach you through your personal accounts, and vice versa. I highly recommend using separate password managers too. You might even consider having two separate phones, to truly keep these aspects of your life apart. I became tired of having two phones so I now use a dual-SIM phone, so much more convenient, but I have to remember to not confuse my work and personal messages and calls.

Virtual private networks

VPNs are another way of hiding your location and where you're logging in from. The VPN acts as a person in the middle, taking your browsing data, encrypting it and running it through a virtual network. Anyone trying to find out where you are will have a tough time, as a VPN makes you appear as if you're somewhere completely different.

There's ExpressVPN or NordVPN, but it's worth looking into the best choice for you. One that you have to pay a monthly or yearly fee for is likely going to be more robust than a free option.

Encrypted messaging

For ultimate peace of mind, you can use encrypted messaging apps, but the chances are you already are. You might have heard the term 'end-to-end encryption', which means only the devices involved in the conversation can decrypt the messages and read them. While in transit, they are virtually impossible to break into, with some so heavily encrypted that government agencies can't crack them.

WhatsApp is an encrypted messaging app, so you're likely already safe from anyone trying to snoop on your private chats. Other apps, like Signal – which also provides an option to set disappearing messages in conversations – are open-source and arguably more secure, and are becoming an increasingly popular alternative to WhatsApp (and are forcing them to provide more security too).

Avoid quick sign-ups

Quick sign-ups might feel more convenient when setting up new social media accounts, but if they're easy for you, they're easy for trolls and fake accounts too. Platforms that use a longer process with some basic ID verification, such as a mobile phone number, mean safer interactions and fewer fake accounts.

Watch your phone security

As humans in the modern age, we're obsessed with 24/7 connectivity. When out and about, it's not uncommon to immediately look for a Wi-Fi when walking into somewhere new. The danger with public Wi-Fi though – especially when logging into an open network that doesn't require a password – is that they make the user an easy target for hackers. Where possible, use public Wi-Fi networks through a VPN. It's worth putting antivirus software on your phone too.

Our phones have **everything** on them. In the wrong hands, you can end up giving away pictures of your loved ones, your bank details, enough personal information to clone your identity, and other content you might not want to share. And if your device was to ever go missing, it's worth having a way to track it and even wipe it. Apple's Find My iPhone or the Android Device Manager are great ones. Also, be wary of being too open with your passcodes in public. It's easy enough for someone to look over your shoulder, learn your passcode and later steal your device.

Regularly review your accounts

Online safety isn't a one-and-done process. It's something you want to set time aside for regularly, at a frequency that suits you. Some people might do it daily; others once a month. There is no one-size-fits-all approach to how often you have to check in on your accounts and online safety, as long as it's enough to make you feel safer and happier online.

Carrying out audits should be a routine part of your online life. Platforms are constantly changing, as are the risks of being online, meaning it's critical to continually check in on where you are and how you're feeling.

I'd recommend setting a bi-monthly 'self-defence reminder' to ensure that you're regularly reviewing your security settings. Personally, I do it every two months **and** just before a big media appearance. Run through all of the steps above and make sure everything is still secure enough for you. It's worth noting that platforms can change their privacy settings at any time, as well as restoring yours to the default when an app updates. Frequent check-ins enable you to catch these changes quickly and reduce any unnecessary risk of harm.

You can switch on automatic security updates for all your devices, which avoids the risk of forgetting. If you see a news article about a data breach in relation to a company you have an account with, be sure to change your password as soon as possible.

There's a brilliant website I love to use – haveibeenpwned.com – that shows you if your information has been compromised. You can add checking this into your regular self-defence routine.

Charlotte Maxwell told me that she's set New Year's Eve as her annual full digital self-care and detox day. A self-described jack of all trades, Charlotte is training to be a clinical psychologist, with a view to specializing in people facing eating disorders and racial trauma.

Talking about her New Year's habit, she said: 'I'm not a fan of New Year's. While everybody else is out having a party, I'm sat there with all my devices set up – I've got a different platform open on each – and I clean them all out. That is my New Year's Eve. And it has been for several years now.'

If you're somebody who's faced abuse in the past, but also hasn't conducted any sort of online audit or implemented any pre-checks, it's definitely worth reviewing your accounts now to identify how and what you would have done differently. That way, for the future, you can implement the tools needed to help you feel safe.

Conduct a risk assessment

For anyone in the public eye, I cannot emphasize enough the importance of performing risk assessments. Think of them as an elevated version of your individual online audit – a practical task undertaken by yourself or on behalf of you by an organization, PR, media specialist or your own team. Like all the other advice so far, this is both digital self-care and self-defence. It's another step in looking after yourself.

Before doing an appearance, any public speaking, or releasing content that could rub antagonists up the wrong way – pretty much anything that's overly public or likely to garner significant attention – make sure to conduct a risk assessment.

The goal of a risk assessment is to consider any and all vulnerabilities, minimizing and managing any risk that a certain job, appearance or piece of press could have on your online safety and comfort. It's about working with your own team, as well as any external teams, to limit the likelihood of abuse happening, and to put support systems in place should it happen anyway.

I've experienced both sides of the coin here.

In May 2021, I made a TV appearance on BT Sport to speak about online violence in the world of sport. Before filming, my team conducted a massive risk assessment. As a result of the risks they identified, I put my block and muting features to good use before going live. BT Sport agreed to regularly moderate the comment section on their social media, particularly YouTube and Facebook. I also used the Block Party app, which automates the moderating of my Twitter feed – something that can be time-consuming to do myself. Apps like this can help filter out content from people you don't want to see and block accounts that retweet or like a bad tweet of your choice by creating, or using others', blocklists. I also had a team ready to look out for abuse and report it as and when it showed up. Those are the steps that allowed me to feel safe and which worked to minimize any fallout from my appearance.

However, I also remember there was one Christmas when I worked on a campaign with Amnesty International. They definitely didn't think to do a risk assessment beforehand, and I soon acquired an abusive stalker – escalating into me being stuck in a lawsuit.

Write for Rights was one of Amnesty's biggest annual campaigns and, in 2018, was intended to encourage Twitter to make their platform safer. Yet, the face of the campaign (me) ended up being abused on the very tool we were calling for action on. All because of an article about the need for them to become safer for Black women.

Amnesty simply didn't know how to support me. And they hadn't put the resources or infrastructure in place to prevent or combat the abuse ahead of time. It was a huge knock to my PTSD and trauma recovery. I then had to be part of teaching an international charity how to do better in protecting their campaign activists and advocates. Once again I had to become my own advocate for solidarity, in the absence of allies and adequate support systems. All of this could have been avoided by them taking a little extra time to perform a risk assessment and predict the potential vulnerabilities that could be exposed.

I spoke about the need for risk assessments with journalist Kat Hopps – who, if you remember, once wrote an article about me that was syndicated and reprinted by other news outlets, ultimately leading to more incessant racial abuse. She reflected on what the experience had offered her in terms of lessons that have stuck with her for the rest of her career.

'With the benefit of hindsight, I could have offered greater support. I definitely could have done more to support you,' she said. 'And I think now, what I've learned is that when you're speaking to people, you should always be completely aware of their background, their culture, or anything that could be a risk factor in them being subjected to abuse online. And to definitely consider who might be vulnerable and how you can try to minimize that through the job that you do.

'I think we also need to remember, at the end of the day, the people we're interviewing are human beings with feelings and emotions, and it can be devastating for them to be subjected to abuse online. We should very much be aware of that and, as a journalist now, what I try to do when speaking to individuals is make sure they fully understand what the interview is about. And, if they were to receive any abuse, make sure I come back and support them however I can. And to perhaps take down comments or remove articles that work to sustain that cycle of abuse.'

So where do you start with a risk assessment for the release of content or an appearance at an event? There are plenty of questions you can ask:

- What boundaries must be respected during and after the appearance?
- Can you opt out of being tagged in any corresponding social posts to minimize your exposure?
- Can they be careful to only tag your professional accounts?
- Who will you be appearing with, or who else will be featured in the article?
- What other information must you know ahead of time?
- Can you reschedule if you're featuring alongside someone of vastly differing views to yourself?

- Does whatever organization you're working with have a team to respond to and report any abuse?
- Do they have a strategy already in place to minimize the impact?
- Do they have someone internally to review comments on your behalf and escalate action where necessary?

With this information, you can take the necessary steps to keep yourself safe. It isn't a guarantee, but you can close off many avenues to online abuse ahead of time.

Document and report

If you have been abused, I do recommend documenting and – if you're comfortable – reporting it. In doing so, you fight to take back some control. Data can also help the police, NGOs and academics identify any patterns, and moves us one step closer to institutionally reducing the scale of online abuse.

Through my own experiences, I've identified huge gaps in the support of victims when it comes to documenting and reporting abuse. Often, those who experience online abuse and harassment are told to ignore it, block it out or censor themselves. Or, even worse, they're told to leave the online space altogether. But if somebody was being catcalled outside the Southbank Centre in London, or somebody attacked me on stage, would you tell us to leave the public space? We cannot afford to be desensitized and complicit in the hijacking of our online spaces. Asking a victim to brush off online abuse or remove themselves from the space is no longer an adequate response.

In light of this, I've created a simple template people can use whenever they experience abuse, no matter how small or seemingly minor the incident might seem in the moment. This way, you have a case ready should you ever decide to report it. There's a link to it in the Resources section at the back of the book. Or you can make your own. What's important is that you report and log your abuse **somewhere**.

Abuse is rarely ever one isolated incident. And by keeping track of abuse as it happens, you remove the emotional labour of trying to piece together painful memories after the fact. You don't have to re-traumatize yourself by compounding all the microaggressions that show the true scale of the abuse you've suffered.

I recommend screenshotting instances of abuse, as accounts and comments can be changed or deleted, and messages can be unsent. Then, upload the images to a spreadsheet with the date, time and website/app/platform where it took place. Most importantly, log how it made you feel in that moment. You might not want to report the abuse straight away. You might prefer to concentrate on healing and documenting allows you to not hold on to the pain. It also allows you to report it more easily should you ever change your mind.

Who you give the report to is, again, up to you. But there are three individuals or groups you might consider:

To the platform

If someone is abusing you online, you can report them directly through the platform they've used – though do keep in mind that a response or action unfortunately isn't guaranteed. While platforms need to do better, as we discussed earlier, reporting is still an important option – and it isn't always hopeless.

There are too many platforms to detail each individual reporting process, but on sites like Twitter, Instagram and Facebook you can click the three dots in the top right-hand corner of someone's post or profile, select 'Report' or 'Report Tweet', and enter your reason for reporting them.

To the police

Where possible, and if you feel comfortable doing so, you can report your abuse to the police. But first, create accurate and thorough documentation of the harassment. This is why it's ideal if you've documented the abuse in real time using a template or spreadsheet. As with my story, be prepared for an emotionally intense experience. Leaning on your community will be vital here.

To your employer, school, parent or guardian

If the abuse happens on a work- or school-related platform, comes from a colleague or peer, or impacts your work, it's important to share what's happening with a superior. We'll dive into what people in these positions should do and what you should expect of them in the next chapter.

By now, you have the self-care advice you need to help you look after your mental well-being, as well as the self-defence tools you can use to stay safe. You're equipped and ready to be a stronger force online, fighting for what you believe in – even if that's just speaking your mind as a woman or a member of a minoritized community. These won't necessarily be easy habits to commit to, and some days will make you feel like giving up, but just know you can always come back to these chapters to get back on track. And remember, I'm here to be your hype-woman.

But this isn't your fight alone. We all need to stand in solidarity with one another, and you'll need allies by your side to support your voice.

Chapter Seven: Collective digital
self-care and allyship

You're in her DMs. I'm in her DMs. We are coordinating a care plan with her consent because community care is crucial during a mental health crisis and helps prevent retraumatization at the hands of oppressive institutions.

Sam Dylan Finch, Twitter, September 2021

In 2021, 1.8 million people suffered threatening behaviour online. But even more people witnessed it. A YouGov survey BT Sport produced with Glitch found that half of the UK population – that's around 33 million people – saw online abuse in some form in 2021. Imagine if all those people had been equipped to do something about it.

Collective digital self-care is about asking how we can be there for each other. How can we build a movement – a community – of understanding and unfaltering support in the face of a digital landscape that presents a very real threat to our health and safety? We have a responsibility as digital citizens to stand against this behaviour and show, without question, that we will do no harm to others. Good digital citizenship is about doing your part to respect and champion the human rights of **all** individuals online.

This chapter is for **anyone**. Friends, family, colleagues, acquaintances. Parents, teachers, employers, journalists. Literally anyone who might ever encounter someone being abused or mistreated online. We can all be better allies to those suffering the impacts of online abuse.

What is digital allyship?

Digital allyship is about providing a place of support, honesty, warmth and understanding – something victims so greatly need when facing online abuse. Being a digital ally is more about supporting the victim than punishing the perpetrator. It might seem easier and a quicker 'win' to call out an abuser. To try to make them apologize or see the error of their ways. But negative language tends to perpetuate the cycle. You want to put your energy into making victims feel seen and heard, and lifting them up instead.

Acting as an ally can take many forms. Allyship includes educating ourselves and others, confronting social injustice if and when we see it – in a productive, calm manner – and listening to and amplifying oppressed voices wherever possible. Allyship is using your privilege to actively support others, especially those who are marginalized.

No matter who we are or where we come from, we can always do something. But it's best if that something is guided by the individual preference of the victim.

For those reading this book because they have faced online abuse, this is why in Chapter Six I encourage you to communicate your online intentions and expectations with those closest to you. That way, if you do ever find yourself a target of online abuse again, your loved ones already know something of how to hold space for you and your healing. It's our responsibility to share with the people closest to us how to act.

And for those reading because they want to be a better digital ally, don't put off these conversations any longer. If you don't know what your friends need from you, ask them. Take notes and keep what they've told you safe. Then, if you see them facing abuse, stand up for them in the way they've asked you to, not how you think you should.

Why we need digital allyship

One of the greatest problems we're currently seeing with online abuse is a culture of passivity. Too many people are standing back and watching individuals get attacked and abused online. While they're not the ones inflicting it, and they may feel empathy for the victim, they're also not exercising any of their power to prevent or minimize the damage. I'm of the opinion that, when it comes to online abuse, silence is compliance. Charlotte Maxwell shared a similar take: 'In some ways, I feel bystanding and doing nothing can almost be a little bit worse.'

Really, when we look at the world both offline and online, we see similar behaviour. If we were to see someone being harassed at work, on the street, on a train or anywhere else in public, we know we should help. We know we should show kindness to that person and support them. But we don't always do that. This is called the 'bystander effect'.

It's a psychological theory that we as people are less likely to help a victim when there are others around – the idea being that 'someone else will probably do something'. It's harmful without us realizing, and it's a difficult effect to overcome. But there are hundreds of stories and videos on the World Wide Web of people stepping up and helping others. It's encouraging to see, and I want to believe it's happening more and more.

Now it's about bringing that same attitude and sense of community to the online space.

Don't judge yourself for falling into the trap of the bystander effect in the past. Just acknowledge its influence and work to fight against it. Work to be a digital ally.

The principles of digital allyship

When I think of digital allyship, the following principles come to mind:

Creativity

Strong allyship is understanding there's no one-size-fits-all approach to showing up for victims of online abuse. As such, allyship involves getting creative in how you let your presence be known and provide support to those suffering, while also centring the victim. It's being able to read the room and identify the best course of action for every unique situation – for those you know and those you don't.

Empathy

Providing a shoulder to cry on, without centring ourselves in the narrative, demands a great amount of empathy. We need to be able to remove ourselves from the situation completely, thinking only of the victim and what they require in the present moment. Empathy is also how we find passion and motivation about the cause, despite not necessarily having experienced online abuse first-hand.

Victim-centred

Allyship should always be victim-centred – no exceptions. Any action you take or choices you make as an ally should be from the perspective of what the victim needs. This isn't about punishing the perpetrators, nor is it about impeding the victim's agency. Rather, you're reinforcing it. Something else it definitely isn't about is getting the clout associated with public solidarity.

Learning and unlearning

Central to being an ally is committing yourself to a lifetime of learning and unlearning. Of accepting your flaws and embracing all you don't yet know. Holding your hands up when you get things wrong and educating yourself on how to do better next time. Strong ally-ship means unlearning any toxic habits you weren't previously aware of, and recognizing any privilege that might presently be going unchecked, then filling the gaps with new, uplifting habits.

Ending the cycle of violence

The ultimate goal of being a digital ally is doing your part to end the cycle of online violence. This is important because there are so many actions that could be considered 'allyship' yet have an adverse effect. They perpetuate negativity and violence, simply displace it, or further minimize or overshadow the voices of the minoritized groups being targeted. Every single mission you undertake as a digital ally should align with the wider goal of shutting down the cycle of abuse, not add fuel to the fire.

Being an ally is complex. Especially an authentic one. It takes time and effort. It takes knowing you won't always get it right. That you'll inevitably do or say the wrong thing from time to time. Despite this, being an authentic ally is an ongoing choice to put in the work and show up for people. To continually learn how best to show solidarity and support, and listen when people tell you how you can lift them up. It's about being an ally because it's the right thing to do, not because it makes you look good on social media.

Allyship on an individual level

How **you** yourself show up as an ally depends on who the victim is, what they want from an ally and your relationship with them.

Personally, I'm not a fan of the empty gesture of 'I'm sorry to hear this. Let me know if there's anything I can do', whether that's from someone I'm close to or a stranger across the world. I'd prefer an ally to bring tangible solutions to the table.

We can all be guilty of scrolling past when we see abuse and hate online. Stopping and being mindful of the abuse means we can start taking action.

For example, you might say (and this depends on your relationship with the victim and what support you're able to offer):

'I've seen X happening to you. I've reported it.'
'I'm coming over to cook for you tonight.'
'Let's head for a walk in the park to clear your head.'

Digital ally tools

Once you move into the mindset of being an authentic digital ally, what do you do next? There's a simple framework you can follow to disarm and reduce online abuse as and when you see it:

1. Spot

Don't dismiss or ignore online abuse. Scroll more consciously in order to be able to respond to the abuse appropriately. Having read through this book, you should start spotting the red flags of online abuse and be in a position to do something about it.

2. Report

If you think an incident of online abuse conflicts with a platform's community standards or terms of service, report it to the platform on the person's behalf. It's relatively quick in most cases, and it's an anonymous action that won't connect you in any way with the abuse or the troll. If appropriate, you can let the individual know privately that you've reported the abuse, so they're aware this action has been taken.

You can also help report the online abuse to the authorities, but keep in mind that not everyone will feel comfortable with that. So get the victim's permission first. If the victim is willing to then you may want to consider offering to go with them. One of the many times I had to go to the police station to give evidence for my case, Rachel – my colleague on the council (who is also a good friend) – supported me; this was so helpful. She didn't know it then, but her privilege as a white woman helped ensure that the police treated my case more seriously than when I'd been on my own.

Another option is to report it to an organization that may be able to provide support, such as the Revenge Porn Helpline, Tell MAMA and the Community Security Trust in the UK. By doing so, you help them capture the scale of the abuse taking place. The Resources section at the back of this book has a fantastic list of suggested organizations.

3. Support

Showing kindness to the person being targeted by online abuse is essential to diffusing the situation. This includes supporting them publicly **and** privately. You can send a kind and encouraging message letting them know you see them and that you're there for them. Even something small like sending a funny meme or an animal picture works (baby videos on Instagram do the trick for me). A little goes a long way in reminding a victim they're not alone.

You can be practical too: document the abuse and take screenshots. This will help ensure it's easier to report. Support and encourage them to document their abuse if they feel comfortable. You can find a helpful guide to documenting online abuse in the Resources section at the back of the book.

If they aren't quite ready to do that, you can send them any resources you've found helpful or relevant. Perhaps something surrounding mental health or self-care. You may also want to recommend they talk to an organization that can provide additional support. In the UK, this might be Samaritans, Victim Support, the National Stalking Helpline, Stand Against Racism & Inequality (SARI) or Galop. But no matter where you are in the world, you should be able to find something similar.

4. Reply

If you know someone is being unfairly targeted in a public post, be their ally by replying to the post as originally intended as if the abuse never took place. Speak directly to them with anecdotal evidence that backs up their point, and steer the conversation back to where it was supposed to be. This helps counter the abuser's attempts at derailing and manipulating the original message. This is best done in combination with sending an encouraging message privately.

5. Amplify

It's important that digital allies actively amplify the voices of those who are targets of abuse. Being a digital ally isn't just intervening when it gets abusive; it's about finding other ways to reclaim our online spaces and set the social norms we should expect of our online communities.

Too often, the view of the person being abused is drowned out, which also isn't helped by allies going on the defensive and further drawing attention away from the point at hand. By echoing the person's sentiments and amplifying their voice instead, we can ensure we still have a diverse range of views in our online spaces. Rather than trying to influence two or three shitty people, inadvertently silencing the original poster in the process, work to raise them up and give them an even bigger voice. (Check out Emma Watson's social media for inspo!)

These are the five steps to being an effective digital ally that Glitch has used to develop training content and workshops for hundreds of people around the world. And Laura Bates echoed my thoughts when she shared her views on digital allyship with me: 'I believe to be an ally, it helps to put yourself in someone else's shoes. When you've been through it yourself, you know what it feels like. If you haven't, you have to do your best to imagine it and think about the impact it would have on every aspect of your life. Recognize that abuse shows up differently for different people.

'One of the bravest parts of being an ally is being prepared to challenge abuse. As citizens of the online space, we get to decide what we normalize and what we challenge. It's a tricky thing, because challenging harm is not always safe to do, and I understand that bringing abuse down on yourself isn't smart, so it comes down to what you can manage and what your power is. There's a white man who has followed Everyday Sexism for over a decade – since the beginning – and when someone comes into our mentions abusing and attacking, often with misinformation, he jumps in and he replies to them. I've no idea who he is. We've never communicated. But I have this huge sense of gratitude towards him. What he does for us is such a relief.

'The expression "don't feed the trolls" is silly. It's not about the trolls. It's about the person who feels stood up for. When it comes to being an ally and supporting others, it's about thinking, "Is there a way I could do something here? Something that would have less of an impact on me than on the person who's experiencing it?" And if there is, then that's a good time to step in. But digital allyship isn't interchangeable with confronting trolls. If confrontation doesn't feel safe, which it doesn't for many of us, it might be about checking in and supporting the person who's experiencing the abuse instead. When someone is being abused, and you genuinely don't know that person or how to help, reach out to say, "I see what's happening to you, are you okay and is there anything I can do?" Something so simple can make a big difference.'

A note on consent

Being a great digital ally also involves the topic of consent. It's something we've made great strides with in the offline world. When it comes to sex and intimate relationships, if we're not agreeing to it, it's sexual assault. Depending on where it happens in the world, it can end in several years in prison and countless lives ruined. Yet, when it comes to data, online behaviour and sharing our personal details and intimate images, we've barely begun to have that conversation on consent.

If you're posting, tagging locations and sharing personal information about yourself, that's fine – it's your choice. But pause and reflect before posting about your friends and loved ones. Especially those from minoritized communities. It might be your profile, but it's their face, their data and their safety. As an ally and – more importantly – as a friend, make sure you know their boundaries and what they're comfortable with sharing online before you make the choice for them.

With that in mind, here are my final tips for being an ally on an individual level.

Tip 1: Minding your own business

Let's normalize minding our own business when we disagree with someone's choices online. It's not always crucial for people to hear 'your truth' – and how much better it would be to do it your way – in the comment section or in DMs. If someone's choices are not harming anyone, let them make their own decisions without your input. Bite your tongue. Write your opinion in your journal or a private group chat if you have to. This is something I have learned to do. Just allow people to live their lives.

Tip 2: Engaging with a perpetrator

Sometimes, you know it's not sensible or safe to openly call out abuse online. But there may be times that it is, and it can be a powerful thing to do.

On striking the balance between being an ally and exacerbating or perpetuating abuse, Charlotte Maxwell explained her thoughts to me: 'It depends how you approach what's gone on. Going in with attacking this person, digging out all their old posts, going to town, it's not appropriate, it's not helpful. It's causing harm to everyone involved. But I think it's okay to simply say "it's not okay to say that". It can be that level of relatively neutral.'

If you're calling someone out online, your goal should be to inject decency back into the situation. To remind the perpetrator how to treat people. That we should all respect universal human rights and you won't stand for anything less.

But remember, you can always walk away. The last thing you want is to create a vicious cycle where calling out a perpetrator sparks a pile of abuse being hurled at them instead. Nobody wins in such a situation. There are just too many people hell-bent on being abusive.

There will also be situations that need a quieter approach. Moments where calling someone **in** when their behaviour is harmful, and educating them privately, calmly and positively through direct messages, for example, might be the best way to go about it.

Here's how the two different tactics look in practice. Calling out is more confrontational. It can end up being performative – more about virtue signalling and appearing more woke than the other person. The goal should be to, in no uncertain terms, let the perpetrator know that what they said crossed a line. Whether they listen and internalize it is up to them. Since we're calling them out, they probably won't. But you are still sending a message, not only to them but to everyone, that you won't stand by and let abuse happen.

While this approach has its place, it's risky. You may not actually be educating the other person, and any apology from them might be calculated and merely to save face.

It's why I think calling in is the preferred tool to take in a heated situation. You turn the aggression into a teachable moment. If you're calling in, you might say something like this:

- 'I just want to know, why did you say what you did?'
- 'What impact do you think your comment had?'
- 'Do you realize how inappropriate the language you used was?'

- 'Did you consider how the other person felt about your comment?'
- 'Why do you see the world this way?'
- 'Where does this come from?'

You're still holding them accountable for their behaviour, but in a way that invites them to be part of the learning conversation and (hopefully) change. It's about recognizing how hurt people often **hurt people**, and that below the surface there might be something driving them to act in such a way. Don't be too quick to get all heated at them, and instead take the time to understand and educate. Should you have to? No – if only people recognized when they were being dickheads. But, as an ally, approaching them in this way can make the world a marginally better place.

This is especially important if you're doing so from a place of privilege. The burden shouldn't be on victims and minoritized communities to explain why something is damaging. If you can use your privilege – say, if you're a white man – to do the explaining, you can take on some of that emotional labour.

While solidarity with the victim is always your best plan of action, it's important to understand what calling out and in looks like, so you can make the best decision on how to handle a situation where you do feel inclined to speak up. Education and defusing a situation, when done correctly, can be extremely valuable.

Tip 3: How to argue

If you do find yourself calling someone out, set a clear intention to achieve a positive outcome for the victim(s). You don't want it to turn into a petty argument, as it often does on social media. It isn't healthy to constantly be in this argumentative state of mind. Not that this is always within our control; the algorithms behind social media push us to speak our minds, even at other people's expense. So what is the appropriate way to engage in an argument?

First, I think it's important not to necessarily look at it as an argument. That implies all parties involved will just be hurling insults at each other. Programmer Paul Graham's 'hierarchy of disagreement' is a great way of viewing these encounters. In his 2008 essay 'How to Disagree' he wrote: 'The web is turning writing into a conversation. Twenty years ago, writers wrote and readers read. The web lets readers respond, and increasingly they do – in comment threads, on forums, and in their own blog posts.' He foresaw that advances in communication and technology would mean an increase in disagreement, and that 'there's a danger that the increase in disagreement will make people angrier' (he was kinda right). So his essay mapped out how to be more careful when disagreeing and ways to do it well.

Graham's 'hierarchy of disagreement' triangle is a helpful resource for recognizing when conversations are disintegrating and heading in the wrong direction. The idea is that, by being aware of the hierarchy, we can improve the argument, actually making salient points and not name-calling.

The latter is actually the lowest level of Graham's hierarchy. You aren't refuting their point by calling them names. If someone were to say 'I think BLM is racist and causes more division', while it might feel good to call them an idiot, you aren't educating them or highlighting that Black lives really do matter. Similarly, ad hominem arguments about their character or attacking their tone aren't helpful.

These are the other bottom layers of the hierarchy. To argue effectively, you want to counter their point, refute it and hit at the central argument they're making. You do this with evidence instead of emotion. In our example, you might say, 'Actually, BLM has helped a great number of Black people air their grievances and start a global conversation on racism that does exist and disproportionately impacts Black communities.' You come at them with statistics that break down their point, not their character.

That person might not listen to you; sometimes, there's no

reasoning with a conscious perpetrator. But **someone** might see what you say and realize they were wrong.

Tip 4: Building people up

Victim blaming is incredibly common when it comes to online abuse. Even those with the best of intentions can end up doing it, without even realizing it. They might minimize the situation, ask a victim what they did to encourage their abuser, and recommend setting their accounts to private, or suggest that they remove themselves from the online space altogether.

Everything you do as an ally should give the victim their agency back, not disempower them further. Don't take major action on behalf of someone without their consent. Instead, try to build them up. Let them know how helpful it can be to have a digital toolkit and the importance of self-care. Validate their feelings, and let them know you're by their side. A helpful validation statement might sound like:

- 'That is hard.'
- 'It's normal to feel this way.'
- 'I'm proud of you.'
- 'It's okay to cry.'

As you become more familiar with the tools and phrases in this book, you'll not only be able to determine how best to handle situations as they arise, you'll find your own creative tools and phrases. To know when to respond to abusive posts yourself and when to encourage victims to report; when it's best to support with kindness and solidarity, and when it's better to encourage someone to take a breather away from the online space and to go through an online audit with them.

Your options for showing up as an ally will constantly grow and evolve as you do. There are so many more ways beyond these pages. If you don't know how to help, then ask people. And always remember, there is no one solution to all forms of abuse. Nor is there one way to be an ally to all people.

Allyship on the community level

In the online space, tech companies paint the picture of us all being part of a 'community'. But this is a bit too nebulous for my liking. In reality, community means being there for people through amazing, joyous times, but also standing by them through the shit times too.

Activist Mia Birdsong wrote a fantastic book, *How We Show Up: Reclaiming Family, Friendship, and Community*. In it, she talks about community as a choice. If you're actively choosing to be someone's friend, you have an active part to play in their life – you're in their ecosystem.

Allyship on the community level means making this conscious choice every day. It means getting to know the people in your chosen and close community (or you may prefer using the term 'extended family') and learning how to be there for them. If you're friends with somebody with diabetes, for example, you're likely to know what to do when they go into diabetic shock. But what about when it feels as if their world is falling apart at the hands of an online abuser?

If we want to shatter the cyclical nature of trauma and violence, it's not enough to keep using the carrot-and-stick method of reward and punishment. We need to replace our old, dated habits and learn and teach new behaviours. We must change the isolated approach of superficial communities, and build intentional collective communities that we **all** make a conscious effort to reinforce. We must all make more of an effort to learn new methods and to educate others on how to be better digital citizens.

One place I'm really keen to see greater community allyship online is interculturally. As Facebook whistle-blower Frances Haugen pointed out, the way algorithms currently work on most

TWO OR MORE THINGS
CAN BE TRUE
AT THE SAME TIME.
THERE DOESN'T HAVE TO BE
TENSION OR
COMPETITION.
SOCIAL MEDIA IS A
TOOL FOR
CAPITALISM
AND LEADING US
DOWN THE PATH
TO EXHAUSTION
AND
IT IS A DEEP PLACE OF
COMMUNITY
AND CARE
FOR DISABLED PEOPLE
AND OTHERS.
IT CAN BE BOTH.

The Nap Ministry, Twitter, 2021

platforms is to feed off outrage. I'm seeing different groups being pitted against one another constantly. This felt particularly worse after Brexit (especially after dogwhistling political statements). It pitted us against one another rather than against systemic oppression, and was doing the work of white supremacists for free.

The online space exacerbates this. But, just like offline, by becoming a digital ally we can demonstrate positive, uplifting intercultural relationships, hold space for each other's communities, and lead the work of anti-racism and liberation for all.

As someone from the Jewish community, human rights lawyer Adam Wagner mentioned finding a similar dynamic within the Jewish and Muslim communities: 'After the New Zealand mosque attack, I put an offer on Twitter that any Muslim organizations looking for free advice surrounding hate and abuse could come to me and I would help. I started organizing events offline at my chamber within the Muslim community . . . I found running those events, going to iftars, and meeting with mosques part of that magic of being part of a different community. It opened my eyes. I met what turned out to be like-minded people from different communities that, apparently, are at war with each other. But, it turns out, we're not. We can offer a lot of help to each other. That's what I want. I want to be cross-pollinating. I want to be an ally. I want to be standing up for other communities as well as my own. Educating others through my personal perspective, but also understanding theirs. By doing that offline, we were able to find common ground online, and stand up for each other.'

Charlotte Fischer, community organizer and co-founder of feminist organization Love & Power, is a fountain of wisdom with whom I often discuss community accountability and allyship both offline and online. She told me: 'Building allyship is not about just being "nice" – and for those who think it is, it often is both a disappointment and short-lived. It's a moral and strategic choice about sharing the risks, and sharing the joy, and strengthening the fight. Solidarity isn't just patronage – it's not based on whether a group will always be there for you, or whether you like them or have ever had a problem with them – it's rooted in the idea that something is happening to a group that shouldn't happen to anyone, but that doesn't take away from the emotional impact of it. It's the relief of feeling that someone else is coming to fight for you. That your community is understood beyond its borders, that someone would stick up for you. It is the converse experience of hate.'

Charlotte believes that allyship both online and offline helps us to understand our own experiences of oppression by recognizing how we are interlinked. 'Those linkages are so crucial – both to understanding how those linkages work, what we have in common, what we have at risk, and how we are played off against one another. Allyship isn't just this annoying thing we have to do, it's that we're building the beloved community we want to see.'

In this sense, the ultimate goal is for community allyship that transcends our pre-existing, close-knit communities, encouraging us to work as an intercultural collective and use our allyship as a way to dismantle oppressive systems both offline and online. Allyship and now digital allyship is fundamental work, because we all need each other. As Charlotte reminded me: 'Bottom line – we're not going to win this on our own. We need our allies.' It's not white versus Black or gay versus straight. It's all of us versus online abuse.

Here are some of my tips for allyship on the community level.

Tip 1: Always bring empathy

Being an ally means truly hearing someone's story and about their struggle. Not inadvertently silencing a victim by brushing them off with sweeping statements, but turning up with empathy instead. We have a real issue as a society, struggling to empathize with each other's fears and especially with women's anxiety of online and offline abuse.

This is something I spoke at length about with Laura Bates. When she was going through her trauma of online abuse people would say, 'You know they're trying to scare you, right?' The implication being: why are you letting this upset you? It's another form of victim blaming. There's a massive disconnect and an empathy gap between society as a whole and the suffering of women and minority groups.

Another example is people maintaining that there's no difference between online abuse for men and for women. That the idea women and minoritized communities suffer from online abuse disproportionately is only a myth.

This lack of wider empathy and understanding is one of the greatest barriers to achieving true allyship on the community level. A big part of the conversation around being a good digital ally and establishing collective communities of support is accepting, first and foremost, that abuse exists. It's real and it's important.

It may never have happened to you, but it doesn't mean it doesn't happen to others. When we deny or ignore the existence of abuse, we only contribute to the problem. We create a barrier for the dickheads to hide behind.

Research shows four in ten people in the UK and US experience online abuse. Let's say those who are committing abuse, spreading toxicity and causing division online make up a small percentage of users. For argument's sake, say it's 5 per cent. While that 5 per cent is still going to result in large numbers of posts and tweets, bystanders still make up the majority. If they all posted a positive piece of content every week, it would drown out the bad actors. Instead of standing by and letting abusers off the hook while ignoring the damage they've caused, let's change the conversation and become digital allies instead.

People buy into the PR around social media too much, believing wholeheartedly that the internet is a community and a safe space and, therefore, online abuse isn't real. Or that it doesn't count. But what about the women and people from minoritized communities who've been killed by people radicalized online? Consider Judge Esther Salas, whose son was murdered and husband seriously injured by a men's rights activist who turned up at her house with a gun and started firing as soon as the door opened.

Of course, plenty of abusive comments are made by people with no intent to follow through on the action. But it only takes one threat with intent to slip through the cracks.

There's every chance you're already fighting the good fight here. And if you are, then great. But now's the time to go one step further and start having these conversations with your wider circles. To educate others and lift them up to your level. To encourage community-wide support and recognition of the very real threat being online presents.

Tip 2: Move past apathy

Another mindset shift we need to go through as a society is to stop diminishing psychological abuse. When Laura Bates went on a high-profile media show, the researcher bluntly told her that viewers do not care about online abuse and she needed to talk about something 'concrete'. Online abuse happens so regularly that we've become desensitized to its existence. Often, this pervasive sense of apathy stops us from pausing to consider whether what we're seeing is wrong. Similar to what I said earlier, we would – I hope – step in were we to see violent abuse happening in our schools, hospitals, train stations or wherever we happen to be. Or at least call the police. But it genuinely worries me that people aren't acting similarly online. Why doesn't online abuse make our blood boil the same way?

As more and more of the world population joins social media, we need more digital allies. Did you know Facebook has 2.89 billion monthly active users? That's about 35 per cent of the entire population of Earth. That's three times the population of Europe. Yet, unlike Europe, Facebook doesn't have a democratically elected government structure, or emergency services. In the absence of legislation and regulations, we need to be that support for each other. Online spaces won't provide all the positive opportunities we know they're capable of if we allow abuse and hate speech to stifle our freedom of expression and erode democracy.

Naming the beast isn't enough. Labelling the abuse is a start, but we can't stop there. It's also about paying attention and having the passion to teach all vulnerable users and the next generation to comfortably navigate the online space without fear of violence. Without fear of victim blaming.

Tip 3: Mindful sharing

Something I've come to learn is that, when trying to support the marginalized online, we can end up traumatizing them ourselves.

Let me give an example. Around the time of George Floyd's murder in 2020, we saw an influx of well-intentioned people sharing the brutality that Black people face, in an attempt to raise awareness. To shed light on incarceration rates and police brutality, as well as wider issues relating to Black Lives Matter and its campaign goals. Seeing these videos countless times, as well as the many arguments with those who 'don't see race', meant it wasn't a joyous time to be a Black person online. Sombre reminders are a helpful wake-up call, but they're also a window to distress and sometimes trauma. Viewing these stories and videos isn't fun at all, and it's a struggle endured over a lifetime. We're not even allowed agency in our online spaces. Whenever we take to our feeds to relax and switch off, there's this lingering anticipation of the next awful piece of news to hit you. We are at risk of being regularly re-traumatized unexpectedly. It's why trigger and content warnings (such as a simple #TW or #CW tag) can be a helpful way to prepare someone for what they're about to see or watch.

As others learn and become activists or campaigners dismantling racism, Black people have to go through the emotional labour again and again. We also see these horrifying events play out over and over offline, and then have it all repeated and discussed for education and 'awareness' purposes online. It's exhausting.

The issue here lies in the content everyone is sharing and how it's impacting their audience. You're going about your day, and suddenly your newsfeed is full of graphic content you weren't ready to see. Posting without thinking isn't abuse. But it can trigger PTSD in those with lived experience, or families that have seen the same harm.

I'm focusing on Black Lives Matter here, but the same goes for stories about homophobia. About transphobia. About misogyny. About online abuse spilling over into offline spaces. These are all incredibly valid. You should also be mindful of what you tag people in or what you share in DMs. Sending a news story of another human rights violation to the community impacted isn't at all helpful. We saw something similar in Chapter Four when talking about unconscious perpetrators; the late Robin Williams's daughter, Zelda, had to ask fans to stop sending her a viral video of someone impersonating her father. They might have assumed it was comforting to see, but really it was opening up old wounds.

Now, this isn't to say we shouldn't educate people and encourage activists to support causes and become a part of the change. But as we incorporate more social media into our activism, we need to be mindful about what's being posted. Is there another way to get the message across? Another way to fight discrimination and abuse? Let's advocate for focusing on liberation, not the injustice.

Tip 4: Organizing online

The final – and perhaps most important – tip is about coming together as a community and pulling towards a common goal. How can we all organize ourselves and make a difference? When you set up a Facebook group, whether it's for your community to come together or for a grass-roots political campaign, how do we make sure leaders have the proper support, advice and nudges to moderate their groups and communities in a safe way?

We can't always be allies on our own. By coming together with other like-minded people, we can combine our efforts and make even more of a difference. How that comes together depends on the community we create. Allies starting an online campaign or moderating an online group should consider the advice given to victims and survivors throughout the book, specifically Chapters Five and Six. These chapters give you an idea of what support they will need, and how you can create a space that allows them to use those tools.

One way people have come together to provide support is through counter-trolling. A concept introduced to me by Laura Bates, it's an interesting idea that I'd love to see more of. Counter-trolls are essentially a team of people who fight back against trolls – not by abusing them in return but by removing their agency and taking away their power.

This can be used to combat 'astroturfing' and 'sock puppet' abuse – when a perpetrator acts as a group of people and tries to dogpile on a community. Astroturf is fake grass, and 'astroturfing' is when an abuser tries to make something look real and grass-roots but it's not. They use lots of fake accounts, all coming out with the same statements to try to suggest that there's a big group online who believe something – but the reality is it's all smoke and mirrors. They can control millions of bot accounts. These fake profiles are called 'sock puppet accounts'.

'Brigading' is described by the *Merriam-Webster Dictionary* as 'a dark tactic of the internet' and is the act of grouping together in order to game a vote and give the impression that the general population swings heavily to one side.

You see these tactics used a lot by male supremacist, anti-feminist groups attacking women – particularly high-profile women. You'll notice a sudden pile-on, where an individual or community faces a wave of abuse seemingly out of nowhere.

In the 2010s, there was an amazing group of women who started a campaign called 'Your Slip Is Showing'. The fact that people don't know about it, I think, is telling. It was a group of Black women who created this incredible way of dealing with brigading – which in this case was an attack on Black feminism by a group of trolls from 4chan. These trolls had started masquerading as Black feminists trying to get

#EndFathersDay off the ground, creating dozens of fake accounts. Their ultimate goal? Trying to turn people against Black feminists – to see them as destroyers of family and community.

What these women did was completely amazing. Bit by bit, they built up this grass-roots defence. After reporting the accounts to Twitter and getting no response or support, they took on the issue themselves. They painstakingly went through the hashtag and found all of the accounts that were suspicious and created a blocklist. They identified images of real women's faces that did not match the names on the accounts, and they shared a blocklist with the world. By sharing #YourSlipIsShowing, they set out to unmask the perpetrators.

If people had paid attention and listened to that huge piece of labour by Black women, then when Gamergate happened a year later (which we talked about at length in Chapter Three), we would have already learned an important lesson in how to deal with it.

Your Slip Is Showing is a little-known story but a great example of real grass-roots activism and solidarity. Women standing alongside each other and saying, 'We're not going to let this happen.' It's proof that if we do stand together, pool our resources, share our blocklists and unmask trolls, we can take away their power. It's a good example of fighting trolls using their own weapons, in a way that we haven't really seen before.

Allyship on the institutional level

Allyship in an institutional sense is about recognizing when you're in a position of power to help someone else. We're talking business owners, employers, teachers, parents, or anyone else in a position of authority. If that's you, then you have the power to elicit real change on behalf of your people.

Talking with Laura Bates, she said: 'If you're a person in a position of power, a person's employer, or have any kind of influence in the particular sphere that [online abuse is] happening in – such as a gate-keeper of a particular online group – take proactive action. You can put rules in place, remove people who are being abusive, and take responsibility for using the power you do have to protect others.'

So what can you do? It might be creating a simple policy that lets your team members know it's okay to step away for a period of time, or that they can pass a social media account they're managing to a colleague if online abuse is becoming particularly triggering or harmful. Or it might be encouraging your students or own children to engage in open conversations if they're finding their time online uncomfortable.

If someone comes to you and they're clearly suffering, cut them some slack. Acknowledge they might need some downtime. Break down that barrier and ask what you can do to help them. Next are some of my tips and processes we both embed at Glitch and support other organizations to embed:

Tip 1: Share resources and tools

Digital allyship is about constantly learning and unlearning. And, when you're in a position of power, you have the privilege of being able to create these critical learning experiences for others.

Encourage healthy allyship by sharing resources you find helpful and inviting conversations around online safety and what it means. Host frequent seminars and presentations people can attend to educate and empower themselves – both on how to handle and avoid online abuse targeted towards themselves, and how best to show up for others.

It's about doing your part to break down this disconnect between online abuse and the offline space, injecting more empathy and understanding into your own organization.

Tip 2: Show solidarity

It's one thing to provide the means for victims to help themselves, but this is about being an **ally**. And that means showing solidarity and standing by them. We saw this in 2021 with John Lewis and their Christmas advert. They publicly acknowledged their duty of care to protect the cast of their advert from racist abuse. The year before, many of the UK's leading supermarkets came together to take a stand against racist online abuse after the backlash to Sainsbury's Christmas ad featuring a Black family. They aired back-to-back adverts with the hashtag #StandAgainstRacism. They made it clear where they stood on the matter.

Another example of a company showing solidarity is Lidl, whose 2019 TV advert for their Irish stores featured a real interracial couple shopping. This drew the attention of the racists, who were quick to aim their vitriol at the couple and their twenty-two-month-old son. Lidl, in no uncertain terms, put out a tweet admonishing the racists and stood by the couple. Their advert had put these people in a vulnerable position, and when there was a backlash they supported them. That's what we need to see more of.

If you're an employer and one of your team tells you that they're being sent inappropriate messages by a co-worker, don't stay neutral. Listen to the victim, take the matter seriously and investigate the case. Don't sweep it under the rug. The problem doesn't even have to be only about internal matters. If a colleague approaches you to say online abuse is affecting their work and mental health, listen to them. Let them know you'll do everything you can to give them the space to get better. There are a growing number of policies around employers supporting workplace victims of domestic abuse, and you can find out more about those in the Resources section at the back of the book.

Having that support from an organization or educational institute – particularly universities – is vital for victims. It's a huge weight off their shoulders.

And show this solidarity publicly. Let it be known that you support victims and that online abuse in any form is unacceptable. Don't make reference to the contents of the abuse, nor include the victim's identity if they don't want it to be known. Where appropriate, amplify their voice and their cause.

Tip 3: Amplify all the time

On that last point, you want to be amplifying minoritized voices even when they aren't being targeted by online abuse. These could be employees, victims, clients, your charity partner or liberation movements. If your staff want to use your influence in the industry to project their thoughts in a larger space, give them that room.

They might want to push a social cause forward, such as Black Lives Matter or LGBTQIA+ rights. Whatever it is, support them in their fight, stand by them, and be ready to take appropriate action if online abuse does come their way.

Tip 4: Using your influence

What other ways can you use your power, outside of giving victims and members of minoritized communities a platform to speak from? Throw your weight around. If you're someone lots of people listen to, ask yourself how you can capitalize on that.

Say a victim of online abuse comes to you, unsure if they want to report an online stalker. They worry it would affect their job performance and that they won't be listened to. You can liaise with the authorities on their behalf. Or you can escalate the issue to social media companies. Anything to take that burden away from the victim.

A few years ago I consulted for an organization that wanted to enter the online gender-based-violence space and one of their issues was that they were aware they had a white, male CEO and founder. My main pieces of advice: to give up space to small organizations, to leverage your much larger platforms and resources to the experts, and to cite, reference, quote tweet and amplify those who have been in the space for several years.

What being an ally isn't

Being an ally doesn't mean being tribal, jumping on the bandwagon of hatred and negativity. It's not throwing all your online etiquette out the window in the name of 'supporting' a victim. It's about injecting decency back into the online space and standing up for what's right in a calm, considered and productive way.

It also shouldn't be performative, to make yourself feel better. Nor should it be about taking action just because everyone else is, or because you fear repercussions from your audience if you don't. It's not something you do for appearances. We saw this with Black Lives Matter in 2020. Plenty of people began sharing black squares, with no real understanding of the complex issue behind them and without any intention of taking further action. This kind of empty solidarity can prevent real change from taking place. At most, it's a nice gesture, but it's not being an ally. It encourages complacency and a false sense of satisfaction at 'helping' the cause. It's not enough. Performative allyship can easily become part of the problem. So take a moment to reflect on where you are lifting people up. Where are you standing by people who need it? How?

In 2021, we also saw an online backlash around Israel and Palestine, with people being attacked for not publicly commenting fast enough on the issue. But we don't want people to speak fast. We want them to speak authentically and sensitively. There's this pressure put on people – especially public figures – to show solidarity within a certain time frame. We believe saying *anything* now is better than saying something thoughtful and considered later. But speaking fast is problematic, because we're inevitably going to make mistakes. We're going to hurt people by saying the wrong thing, because we haven't waited to properly educate ourselves or gather all the facts.

We exist in an instant culture where everything has to happen yesterday, and everyone is expected to have an opinion on everything. But then we're also quick to attack people when they do get things wrong or make a mistake. It's a lose-lose scenario.

Speaking with human rights lawyer Adam Wagner, he feels similarly: 'I feel so much of Twitter is empty gestures. I no longer feel comforted by people saying to me publicly, "I'm sorry to see what you're going through," because it makes me feel like a victim. I also feel patronized and it's hard to explain without sounding callous. I feel it's falling into the Twitter trap of everything being team-based, all about who you support and who you disagree with . . . And it's as if you have to respond to everything. You must respond the minute something happens.'

Public declarations aren't the only way you can show up as an ally. The pressure of 'if I don't say something, people will ask me why I'm not saying it' is part of the reason for inauthenticity and feeds this toxic (and addictive) culture of urgency.

This pressure to speak out also exists when it comes to calling out abuse or problematic behaviour. We can feel such pressure to fit in and stick with our designated tribes online. And we can end up responding to online triggers – jumping on the bandwagon of calling someone out – without even considering what we're reacting to or for. We end up contributing to public shaming, lashing someone online – sometimes even *after* they have come out and apologized for their mistake. At this point, we're just being an unconscious perpetrator and adding to the problem.

Jameela Jamil explained it to me like this: 'The thing I want most people to know is that if someone has done something wrong, check the comments section before you contribute your opinion. Maybe it's already been said 100,000 times. Ask yourself: who are you doing this for? Are you doing this for the person that has made a mistake, or are you doing this to announce yourself as still within the tribe?'

There's this pressure to be an ally for the sake of it – or to avoid being criticized for not saying anything or taking a stand. Silence has become the new cause for violence, in a way. But there's a distinct difference between appearing to be a digital ally to gain likes and retweets and being an authentic ally. Publicly tweeting what effectively amounts to 'U OK hun?' isn't enough any more. Neither is dogpiling on someone who made a mistake after they've been told a million times and have already apologized. As a community we need to genuinely show up. And not only online, but offline too.

In our conversation on this subject, Adam Wagner also said: 'When the Sarah Everard case was prominent, I made an offer on social for women having problems with the police to give me a call and I would advise them for free and set them up with the right team if needed. That's what led to the Reclaiming the Streets case and we went to court. It was the same for the shooting in the mosque. I thought, "Sod this, no more public displays of emotion. I'm going to offer something and I'm going to do something." I mean, it's not perfect, I'm only one person. But I've got some power, I recognize that power, and I'm going to use it. I don't think my power is in influencing people. Yes, I can influence people, but I think it's a pretty soft power. My power is being able to help, so that's what I set out to do.'

Do the work offline

Being an ally online is only one part of the fight. The online space is a continuation of what we see offline. Everything that holds women and minoritized communities back in the world exists offline too; it's impossible to separate one from the other. So if you're doing the work online, you need to be doing it offline too.

We cannot talk about online allyship and how to be a responsible digital citizen without understanding how we do that offline. Everything you learn in this chapter is something you can apply to every facet of your life. Don't just call in (or call out) people online; do it at work or with your mates in the pub (as well as in the group chats). Don't just stand by people on Twitter; stand by them when someone shouts at them on the street.

What we desperately need is progressive political education that focuses on decolonizing our curriculum so we learn the facts about race, sexism and other forms of systemic oppression. But we don't have that yet. So, for now, we all have to be the change we want to see in the world. Let's all be clear about where to draw the line between abuse and public accountability. Because when we do this online **and** offline, we can start to see the difference we want.

Digital citizenship

At the end of the day, we're all digital citizens. And it's the responsibility of all of us to build and maintain the online spaces we want to exist in.

Digital citizenship is about making sure that we engage positively and responsibly in all digital spaces. It's recognizing that we all deserve to safely and freely engage online without fear of harm or discrimination. It's respecting and championing the human rights of **everyone** online – not just ourselves or people like us. It's a responsibility on the individual, community and institutional levels to do better. To be respectful, and do everything in our power to avoid inflicting or inciting harm on others.

Being a good digital citizen is recognizing how some actions cause more harm than good – even when you have good intentions. If you have a large audience online and retweet something, are you amplifying something negative accidentally? Have you retweeted without a moment's thought, or have you double-checked the context? Your amplification can bring with it attention – which can be a wonderful help – but when it's an individual's account, take an extra minute to be mindful and conduct a quick and caring risk assessment for the person whose profile you're raising. It's been lovely to read DMs from people with a whole lot more followers than I have asking if it's okay to repost or amplify my content.

Digital citizenship has two layers: hard and soft. The harder, compulsory behaviours include being mindful that you're not sharing misinformation or negativity. Taking the time to fact-check whatever you're putting out on your platform. The soft layers of digital citizenship are more about the human element of the online space. Not all internet use is mindless scrolling. It's taking a minute to stop and consider the human behind the screen name. If you have someone in your community who is always consistent but they haven't posted in a while, or they seem a little bit off, take notice. Reach out to them to make sure they're okay. The softer side of digital citizenship and being a digital ally is about creating a caring, collective space for people, and actively choosing to serve a real, tangible purpose in people's lives.

If we all had five to ten people in our squad, then everyone would be cared for. Fewer people would slip through the cracks. And if you're going to be in someone's community, be genuinely in it. How are you supposed to hold space for someone when you don't truly know them? Collective care and self-care are equals when it comes to tackling online abuse. They work in tandem with one another. When you're okay, I'm okay.

It's our responsibility as a collective to stop algorithms from feeding into hatred. Posts only go viral when people jump on the bandwagon. If we can collectively recognize when something has the potential to cause harm, the algorithm will have to move on to something else – hopefully promoting positive content instead. One individual cannot impact the algorithmic beast. However, a collective of individuals thinking conscientiously? Taking their digital citizenship seriously? That's where the real magic begins.

It only takes a few simple changes for us all to become better digital citizens and allies. We can build uplifting online communities that provide genuine support and care. We can use our privilege to uplift those who are silenced or minimized. We can stop perpetuating harm accidentally. We can be proactive and help reduce the risk of abuse. And we can constantly learn and unlearn alongside one another, gradually moving towards safer, more empowering online spaces for all.

Chapter Eight: Mistakes and reflections – what my journey so far has taught me

If you'd told me in 2017 that I'd be the accidental CEO of a UK charity in my late twenties, pioneering change in the online space and writing this book, I would have seriously laughed at you. Go back even further and tell me in the nineties that this East Londoner would be an outspoken voice in the tech space, and I wouldn't have even known what the tech space was.

But, ever since 2017, life has been a whirlwind for me. Founder and CEO of Glitch, attending high-level meetings with policy-makers and senior leaders of tech companies in the UK, Geneva and New York, and helping to change policies and legislation. I've delivered training to thousands of people and allies across the globe, with some of my favourite times being on the continent of Africa. I've developed resources, with one translated into Portuguese to support Afro-Latinx people across Brazil. I've done countless fascinating interviews with celebrities and strong female and minoritized voices, including for the front cover of *Wired*. I've won multiple awards and even undertaken a Fellowship at George Washington University. And I've provided extensive briefing papers for celebrities and Members of Parliament alike.

All of this has led me to write this book for you.

In the spirit of raw honesty and transparency that has shaped this book and my expertise, I couldn't end without sharing my mistakes and reflections. Social media wants us to put on a happy face and share our highlights, propping up the dangerous narrative of perfectionism. Dangerous because, as humans, we're not perfect. Nor should we feel the pressure to be.

Intersectionality, lived experience and inclusive feminism have been guiding frameworks for how I approach my work. They enable me to see who's not in the room, the experiences and communities not being discussed, analyse power dynamics, and identify how to address this equitably.

Learning, unlearning and making mistakes are important to highlight. We should all be encouraged to share and wear the badge of 'recovering dickhead' with pride. But that's what life's all about; there's no 'end goal'. Rather, it's a series of lessons that lead to change. This principle is particularly important when heading up an organization or running a campaign. It's only through learning that we can be truly inclusive. And this is a principle we need in our online spaces – even more so to counter the algorithms exploiting our outrage and emotions.

Trauma-informed work

In Chapter Two, I shared the experience of online abuse that led me to set up Glitch. It was a traumatic time, shaping a very personal and sometimes narrow relationship with tech and gender rights. In the moment, I was angry. In a sea of anonymous troll accounts, all I wanted was for every single harasser to face justice, while knowing full well that wouldn't happen. Existing in that mindset for so long took a toll on my mental health. My response to my trauma was going into fight mode.

When I finally took a few days to rest, my body seized up. It was as if I was training for an Ironman. I was in a constant state of burnout from the incessant fighting, PTSD and having to retell my story over and over again, and I was beaten down. Because of that, I

STOP TURNING

PAIN

INTO A CAREER.

GO HEAL

AND FACE THE PAIN FIRST

BEFORE YOU
MAKE IT YOUR
SOLE IDENTITY.

Adéọlá Adérèmí, Twitter, June 2021

took a two-month break. I realized I was being led by my trauma. I was paranoid and fearful, and wasn't sleeping or eating well. In campaigning for liberation and freedom for other women online, I didn't take the time to do some much-needed healing for myself.

It wasn't healthy. But it taught me the importance of acting from a position of being trauma-informed, not trauma-led.

Embracing anger as women is so crucial for personal growth as well as long-term community organizing and building. Science points to the damage that anger, stress and surviving on adrenaline does to our bodies. And this damage impacts our ability to do the work of collective self-care and systemic change.

Being trauma-led is acting as a direct **result** of your trauma and using it as fuel, rather than letting your traumatic experience (and those of others) help shape and inform your strategy and delivery. Being trauma-informed means you have an understanding of the trauma that's affecting you. Instead of acting immediately, you take everything on board, process it, and act later in a thought-out, considered manner. It means understanding a situation fully and not operating in fight-freeze-flight mode, but rather with some distance and from a position of wanting to do the right thing.

Hurt people hurt people. I've seen campaigners who have survived violence perpetrating that violence against other minoritized individuals or groups. This cycle of violence is infecting feminist movements, liberation movements and our society at large.

My trauma-informed position means I still support others and provide insight for both policy-makers and tech companies. But without being re-traumatized.

I prioritized my self-care to make sure I wasn't a risk to myself or my team. This involved seeking counselling and mental health support. Turning trauma into activism is therapeutic, but it's not therapy. I did one year of intense CBT to retrain my brain. Months in, I noticed a change within me, but also in my approach to work and my professional relationships with others.

Granted, this is much harder in countries where therapy isn't free or easily accessible. If that's the case, create a community for yourself or seek one out. Form a peer support network, or look to the people who can help your healing the most. I follow a ton of great trauma-healing professionals on Instagram, for example. (Make sure you check their credentials.)

If you've birthed a campaign, organization or a career from your trauma, I strongly encourage you to set up your own accountability framework and network. If you're engaging in activist work, there's plenty of behind-the-scenes and inward work you must continue to do.

I'm constantly reflecting and finding that balance between my trauma being this experience I've been through and also the inspiration to do something with it. Being trauma-informed instead of trauma-led is a tricky line to walk with Glitch, which was born from a very real experience for me. It's a constant battle, requiring reflection, my friends holding me accountable, and protecting my well-being and the sustainability of the organization. Never forget that we are all more than our trauma.

Anonymity isn't always bad

For a long time, I believed anonymity was a bad thing online. That being anonymous was you wearing a mask. And that you have to show yourself and be who you are online. I now realize that this is a reductive view, and that much more nuance is needed. I recognized further down the line that this was me approaching the subject from a trauma-led perspective, as everyone who had abused me was anonymous or using a fake account. I couldn't find out who they were, so I believed that anonymity to be bad.

Over the years of speaking to feminist activists – especially in India, Latin America and Kenya – I realized that for some people access to anonymity is essential for their safety and the sustainability

TRAUMA
OFTEN LOOKS LIKE
FREEDOM.
TRAUMA SEEKS
REPETITION.
THIS MUST BE PART OF THE
CONVERSATION.

Guilaine Kinouani, Twitter, November 2020

of their work and livelihood. It was the only way these women could ever hope to fight against oppressive regimes. Remember that, even in the UK, Azmina had to change her surname after launching the *#ToxicTwitter* report.

Looking through an intersectional lens, in certain countries where women are still deemed second-class citizens, anonymity helps them express themselves as freely as a woman in the West might be able to. The transgender community is another that benefits from the ability to create anonymous profiles, as a stepping stone to their true identity or for protection. The world isn't an inclusive place yet, so it's understandable why some people need anonymity.

In all these cases, these are people going against the power and the status quo. Anonymity is a shield for marginalized people, freedom fighters, whistle-blowers, and people sharing a #MeToo experience. Anonymity is a human right. It's an extension of freedom of speech.

It's unfortunate that it's a right that's been abused and co-opted by bad actors so they can spout hateful rhetoric with no repercussions. But removing people's access to anonymity isn't going to change the world. Look at former president Donald Trump. He was only banned from Twitter and Facebook in 2021, after *years* of extremely inappropriate and harmful behaviour. And he did so with his full name in view – no secrets, no masks. Just pure, unadulterated him. So it's naive to believe that removing anonymity will cause online abuse to disappear. One thing we can do as users is to decide whether or not we're going to interact with anonymous accounts or mute or ignore them. It can form part of the page policy we discussed in Chapter Five.

That the concept of anonymity has been stolen is terrible. It robs people of their agency and is often used as a tool to oppress already-marginalized communities. But removing anonymity can only hurt the already hurt. It's why I love the work of the likes of Yoti, a company that provides secure identification that is especially helpful for young people who don't have access to passports or provisional licences. It is an encrypted, safe way of being verified, and it's secure: no one other than the user can access that data. Could this idea be used on a wider scale to protect even more people?

There has been some debate around whether requiring ID verification when setting up social accounts could be the way forward. Now, I'm not so sure I agree with the sentiment. If this were the case, how could an LGBTQIA+ person still in the closet explore their identity online without their family knowing? How could women access education in places where they're technically not allowed to? Is there a way to allow for these exceptional circumstances?

Anonymity and online abuse are not mutually exclusive. Instead of believing 'anonymity = bad', I've instead switched my view to 'using the privilege of anonymity to be a dickhead = bad'. I realized that, by blaming anonymity, I **wasn't** blaming what was really at the heart of it: white supremacy and the patriarchy. Now I don't obfuscate that conversation, and I make sure my attention is squarely where it's needed.

Punitive measures aren't always the answer

In the early days, I thought prosecuting all perpetrators would be a great deterrent to others. That it would inspire better, more positive online behaviour and give the victim a sense of justice. It was through speaking to amazing organizations in the Global South, such as the Association of Progressive Communications, as well as through retreats, training and reading, that I realized this was a very dangerous perspective to have.

Abolition campaigners made me reflect on my own organization. I look back now and realize that prioritizing prosecution would be creating a pipeline to prison. And that's a system that's easily abusable by a government that wants to do so, putting the privacy and security of all of us at risk. While the Black Lives Matter movement might be about the unjust deaths of Black people at the hands of police, it's also about the sheer number of Black people who are put in prison for minor offences a white person would get a slap on the wrist for. Didn't it make me a hypocrite to want to condemn so many people to extreme imprisonment? Especially in a system that doesn't focus enough on rehabilitation? How rehabilitating is prison for a fourteen-year-old who didn't have comprehensive relationship and sex education? My original belief held a lack of compassion for the social ills that cause people to inflict harm and damage.

Taking a public health approach to understanding the drivers behind people committing abuse would enable more effective preventative measures, lightening the burdens faced both by victims and by organizations such as the NHS that have to deal with the impact that abuse is having. A wider educational conversation around our online responsibilities, as well as what social ills drive online abuse, is more effective than legislation alone for understanding and 'fixing the glitch'. With mental health struggles behind a significant amount of online trolling, taking this approach could provide the preventative actions we need to avoid online abuse.

Part of this is looking at who the trolls are. There's this stereotype that they're all greasy angry men living in their mums' basements. This is far from true. In 2019, one troll on the Tattle Life forum was caught creating a fake account to abuse friends, Black women, guests on podcasts and even her own husband. But this troll was a woman who, outside of her online activities, was just living a normal life. She wasn't the stereotype, but she was doing damage all the same. Yes, there are incel groups who very much foster a collective hatred of successful women. But as the Tattle Life story shows, our twenty-first-century online trolls also include our 'faves', our political leaders and maybe even our friends and work colleagues – many of whom have faced their own share of trauma.

The social ills that cause these perpetrators to act like dickheads online aren't being tackled and, as a result, the internet is a petri dish for toxic behaviour. Once we understand what's missing, and what the root causes are, we can begin to allocate funds and work to improve these areas.

We need a solution that gives victims a sense of justice and allows them to move on, while also showing a degree of compassion and understanding for perpetrators, offering opportunities for rehabilitation. A public health approach to youth violence is a methodology advocated by the World Health Organization (WHO), and in Scotland it had a tremendous positive impact on breaking the cycle of violence. Since 2008, the Scottish government has funded several programmes and initiatives including the Scottish Violence Reduction Unit, and it is internationally recognized as being at the forefront of our approach to preventing violence. It's an inspiring story that shows it does work.

Not everyone who behaves badly online should go to prison. I don't think that's going to solve the issue or end online abuse, but equally any solution shouldn't be at the expense of the victim. The two truths can exist. Not all abuse is equal, and the punishment should be appropriate. Ian Wright, the ex-footballer and now TV presenter, made a choice to forgive an Irish teenager who sent him abusive private messages on Instagram. He made a public status of 'I'm moving on, all is forgiven, leave it to the courts'. When the judge picked up the case, because Wright had forgiven him publicly, he felt there was no need to give any sentence to this young boy or ruin his career. Wright was disappointed there wasn't harsher punishment, but the case for him had still never been about revenge, it was about 'consequences for acts of racism'.

The challenge with this outcome was that the judge entirely dropped the case and removed any access to justice for the victim. This sent a message that the perpetrator shouldn't have been punished for the abusive behaviour, which wasn't going to solve the issue either.

We need clearer legislation around what is and isn't abusive and harmful behaviour, and what won't be tolerated. Once we have this, we can look at creative ways to achieve restorative justice and address why people become perpetrators in the first place. Isolation, poverty, self-esteem and mental health issues are all contributing factors outside of being down-and-out racist, sexist and so on. Once we set standards for the behaviours that we want to see online and instil accepted social norms, then we can establish what appropriate punishment should look like for those not respecting those boundaries. There are so many steps you can take before imprisonment, such as de-platforming.

It's also about liberation, to experience joy

My response to women being sent death threats is to push for the police to take victims more seriously. For policies to be more inclusive and intersectional. For tech companies to do more. I and many others fighting violence against women, girls and minoritized communities are so focused on the harm. However, the abuse is only half of the story.

Of course, I want women to feel safe. To **be** safe. But this is the bare minimum. More than that, women should be able to flourish online and experience freedom. Let's move from being able merely to survive online, and escalate the conversations to be about women and minoritized communities **thriving** online. We should be able to express ourselves and make mistakes. We should be able to talk about our periods without being shadowbanned on Menstrual Hygiene Day because the discussion is deemed to be 'pornography'. To talk about cancer and all the other causes that matter, without platforms perpetuating conservative patriarchal ideology and telling women what is and isn't acceptable when it comes to their bodies.

When I talked to Jan Moolman from the Association for Progressive Communications, she described the power that imagination has in forging our future online spaces. You might remember her from the very start of the book; she's the woman who took me under her wing several years ago and set me on the path I'm on today.

She told me: 'There's something about imagination that is so essential and productive for our movements. For any movement working on violence. Any social justice movement. Imagining what our lives can be if all of the shit is gone. And believing that it can be . . . I don't want to be resilient. I want to be who I am all the time . . . It's important to remember why we are doing this. Yes, it is to end violence against women. But essentially, it's about creating a life where we are free. The thing for me about technology when I first started was the idea of being whoever I wanted to be on whatever day it was.'

I'm happy and proud of the changes we at Glitch, our partners and others in the ecosystem have made in tackling online violence, and we have so much further to go. But I want to set my sights on a much bigger, more positive outcome. The majority of Glitch's funds thus far have been spent on survivors of online abuse. Moving forward, I'm widening my focus to include helping women and minoritized communities to thrive and flourish online too. To not only be safe, but to be free.

Let's end online abuse, while also taking it a step further and creating a world where everyone has the freedom to exist fully and authentically online.

Online safety in the workplace is critical

I'm not sure how this reflection will age. But, at the time of writing, it's a particularly pressing concern.

During the first COVID-19 lockdown in 2020, we saw our online and offline worlds merged together even more so than ever before – and arguably irreversibly too. What was once done offline was now innovatively done online. It was how we worked, stayed in contact with friends and family, bought our groceries, entertained ourselves, celebrated culture, explored new places and learned new things. To keep us connected to one another and retain some modicum of a 'normal' life, we needed the online space more than ever before. And I don't think our offline/online balance will ever be the same as a result.

It wasn't just about social media. It served as a stark reminder to rethink our digital self-care when it comes to work. No one was prepared for the dramatic shift. Bedrooms and kitchen tables were converted into offices. Desks, chairs and computers crammed into spaces. Employers frantically furnishing homes with stronger broadband. Tech avoiders trying to figure out how to use Zoom and Teams to connect with their team. It was chaos. And, as our connectivity increased, so did our direct access to harm.

There was hardly any guidance on how to handle the change. No one seemed to know what to do. But now we **need** to figure it out. Artificial intelligence research company ASAPP found that 81 per cent of call centre agents experienced customer abuse, with 36 per cent threatened with violence, and 21 per cent of female call centre agents were sexually harassed. In addition to the abuse staff receive from customers, how do we handle inappropriate contact between members of staff who now have a window into each other's homes?

We don't yet have a full understanding of the impact of online abuse, including longitudinal studies of minoritized communities. And we certainly don't have a full understanding of how the impact of online abuse has been amplified by the COVID-19 pandemic. I think we're yet to see the backlash to this dip in safety, and the real impact will start to show in two to three years. Depending on when you're reading this, it might already have come to light. But I predict it's going to appear most in issues around mental health and well-being. I believe there's going to be an increase in demand for better policies around online health and safety. As I said in Chapter Four, governments and tech companies will need to start prioritizing people's safety and well-being in online spaces, with increasing pressure being put on employers to provide adequate support and understanding.

Milestones

To date, compassion – specifically self-compassion – has been the most difficult principle to learn and live by. Learning (and sometimes unlearning) from teachers like Tara Brach and The Nap Ministry, as well as podcasts, my therapists and friends (who have been telling me to be easier on myself for years) in the autumn of 2021 has done wonders for my soul, and encouraged me to revisit this chapter in early 2022. To find balance in my reflections, and not just point out the mistakes but also give space and attention to the milestones, the proud moments and the things I did get right.

This brings me to my final reflection: learn to love and be kind to yourself. In this world that feels cruel and more isolating every year, developing an authentic and loving relationship with ourselves is crucial to thriving not just surviving. How to be present, and how to breathe and listen to my body – ensuring body and mind are in sync – are the most liberating life lessons I am learning. And these are for everyone, but especially for leaders (founders, to be even more specific) who feel like they don't have the time. You do.

I'm most proud of my feminist leadership and management (you quickly learn the difference between the two when running an organization). I'm proud of my inclusive approach to addressing online abuse – who we collaborate with and who we centre in policies and advocacy. Finding the balance in being an independent and critical friend of tech companies – fair and brave – while acknowledging all the other drivers of online abuse. I'm proud of embedding a feminist-values approach in Glitch, and the growth of my small but mighty team. We have done some unimaginable and life-changing work for an organization that only became a charity in 2020 and started as a small campaign on my personal website in April 2017.

And so we're at the end . . .

Let me close by repeating that the online space can be a brilliant and empowering place. All this talk of abuse can make us focus only on its negative aspects, but it's important to remember a number of truths can coexist. The internet has made the world smaller, allowed us to connect, start movements, support projects, listen to and empathize with others, and spread our ideas, creativity and stories all around the world. But the positives of our digital world cannot overshadow the other truths: the harms and violence that are hijacking our online spaces. That technology is yet another instrument in upholding systems of oppression, and that we need to end the silencing of victims and the growing numbers of people who aren't able to flourish online. This book was written to shine a light on these other truths that have gone unaddressed for too long.

The advice, stories and recommendations in these pages make up the first phase in how we can all stay safe online. It's the beginning of dismantling those instruments, giving a voice to victims who have been ignored, and upskilling ourselves as digital citizens. I call this phase of our mission 'tackling the monster of apathy'.

It's apathy that means our society has a warped and unhealthy tolerance for online abuse. Apathy has a domino effect online and offline and on those disproportionately impacted. Being apathetic towards ourselves and others when it comes to online violence comes from not understanding the magnitude, and a lack of inspiration in terms of what the future of technology can and should look like. We deserve a sense of duty of care and the prioritizing of safe design from tech companies, and protection and leadership from our elected representatives. And sharing knowledge and digital self-care and self-defence tips with others while being proactive not only breeds greater empathy, it empowers individuals and strengthens communities. It prepares us for phase two of our mission and a future conversation, a radical and global conversation – full systemic change.

In the meantime, I hope this book not only sparks conversations and informs but also sparks imagination and new (inclusive) possibilities among families, friends and colleagues. I also hope these conversations happen within places of power – in government and tech companies. Then hopefully we will become ignited to change the status quo, to challenge the rhetoric of withstanding abuse, and to not inadvertently be someone else's perpetrator. We should be excited to create online environments with common values, and develop social norms that enable all of us to evolve, flourish and, importantly, feel safe online.

Acknowledgements

I first want to thank my mum, Aramide, and my boyfriend, William Oppon, and all my friends, for bearing with me as I was growing my first baby Glitch while also birthing a new baby with this book. Thank you for putting up with my tiredness and the occasional tears (Hannah Stevens), for sending cute baby content and meeting my desperate need for bottomless brunch (Jess and Tanda) and fun nights out (in between lockdowns).

Thank you, Rachel Tripp, for holding me accountable and giving me some of my first-ever book-writing advice. To Laura Bates, for encouraging me to write a book and guidance on writing a book proposal (oh, and sending me gin!). To Anna Codrea-Rado, Laila Woozeer and Alex Holder from the More than Money WhatsApp group, for lending your wisdom about the book-writing process to a debut and scared writer – thank you sincerely for your vulnerability. To Gabby Jahanshahi-Edlin and Rebecca Bunce for reminding me of my own self-care principles when I'd often forget and for affirming my boundaries (and Gabby, thank you for pushing me to negotiate a good book contract and being a great co-founder of the More than Money group). To Ray Murphy for hooking me up with Sonder & Tell, and helping me develop my voice and a brand distinct from Glitch. To the Black womxn (Martha Awojobi, Mutale Nkonde, Ronda Železný, Nova Reid, Deborah Okenla, Edafe Onerhime, Nani Jansen Reventlow, temi lasade-anderson and Carys Afoko) who held me during the summer of 2021, one of my lowest and depressing leadership moments. To all of you who reached out for coffees, love-bombed me in WhatsApp chats (Janey Starling) and groups, and helped me find joy again.

To my therapist – God bless you and your patience with me. To all those I dance with on weeknights and my dance teachers – thank you for creating safe and joyful spaces. To Alix Dunn, Asha Allen and Hera Hussain, who read my draft manuscript when I was burned out and my confidence was so low it was kicking my arse! Thank you to everyone who gave up their time to be interviewed for this book – I thoroughly loved all of our conversations. Thank you to team Glitch and all Trustees for giving up your time to help get this charity off the ground with such little money in the bank and with limited funding connections. Glitch team old (Lauren Pemberton-Nelson, Rachel Grocott, Luke Dwyer and Chas Ochalek) and present (Eva – you saved my sanity; Gabriela, Gwen, Hilary, Chris, Zahabiya and Caitlin), I love working with you! To my executive assistants over the years (Laura Kay, Sharon Panayiotou) and now (Kayleigh and Sharmaine), for protecting my time and energy in my diary – especially my Fridays for writing this book.

I finally want to acknowledge all the amazing women and girls who have also survived online harms, and all those who are working tirelessly to make our digital spaces safe, equal and inclusive.

References

Introduction

Women's Media Center, Speech Project, https://womensmediacenter. com/speech-project.

Statista, 'How often do you see internet trolling on the following types of media?', https://www.statista.com/statistics/379997/internet-trolling-digital-media/.

Amnesty International, 'Troll Patrol Findings', https://decoders.amnesty. org/projects/troll-patrol/findings.

United Nations Human Rights Council, 'Human Rights Council holds Panel discussion on online violence against women human rights defenders', 21 June 2018, https://www.ohchr.org/EN/HRBodies/ HRC/Pages/NewsDetail.aspx?NewsID=23248&LangID=E.

Glitch UK and the End Violence Against Women Coalition, *The Ripple Effect: COVID-19 and the Epidemic of Online Abuse*, September 2020, https://glitchcharity.co.uk/wp-content/uploads/2021/04/Glitch-The-Ripple-Effect-Report-COVID-19-online-abuse.pdf.

Centre for Community Organizations, *White Supremacy Culture in Organizations*, November 2019, https://coco-net.org/wp-content/ uploads/2019/11/Coco-WhiteSupCulture-ENG4.pdf.

Chapter One: Why this book shouldn't need to exist

Mark Townsend, 'Plymouth man ranted online that "women are arro-gant" days before rampage', *Guardian*, 14 August 2021, https://www.

theguardian.com/world/2021/aug/14/plymouth-gunman-ranted-online-that-women-are-arrogant-days-before-rampage.

Plan International UK, 'Girls' Rights Are Global', https://plan-uk.org/file/10-point-plan-global-girls-rightspdf/download?token=N4sKR9Av.

Sydette Harry, 'Listening to Black Women: The Innovation Tech Can't Figure Out', *Wired*, 11 January 2021, https://www.wired.com/story/listening-to-black-women-the-innovation-tech-cant-figure-out/.

Rachelle Hampton, 'The Black Feminists Who Saw the Alt-Right Threat Coming', *Slate*, 23 April 2019, https://slate.com/technology/2019/04/black-feminists-alt-right-twitter-gamergate.html.

Ashley Reese, 'Talib Kweli's Harassment Campaign Shows How Unprotected Black Women Are Online and Off', Jezebel, 4 August 2020, https://jezebel.com/talib-kwelis-harassment-campaign-shows-how-unprotected-1844483551.

TrollBusters, http://www.troll-busters.com.

Chapter Three: How to define online abuse

Stonewall, *School Report: The Experiences of Lesbian, Gay, Bi and Trans Young People in Britain's Schools in 2017*, June 2017, https://www.stonewall.org.uk/school-report-2017.

BT Sport, 'It's Time to Draw the Line', https://www.bt.com/drawtheline.

Statista, 'Numbers of anti-Semitic incidents reported to Community Security Trust (CST) in the United Kingdom from 2004 to 2020', https://www.statista.com/statistics/383740/antisemitic-incidents-reported-uk-y-on-y/.

Greg Elmer, Anthony Glyn Burton and Stephen J. Neville, 'Zoom bombings disrupt online events with racist and misogynistic attacks', *The Conversation*, https://theconversation.com/zoom-bombings-disrupt-online-events-with-racist-and-misogynist-attacks-138389.

Charlotte Alter, 'UN Says Cyber Violence Is Equivalent to Physical Violence Against Women', *Time*, 24 September 2015, https://time.com/4049106/un-cyber-violence-physical-violence/.

Amnesty International, 'Troll Patrol Findings', https://decoders.amnesty.org/projects/troll-patrol/findings.

Brené Brown, 'Shame vs. Guilt', 15 January 2013, https://brenebrown.com/articles/2013/01/15/shame-v-guilt/.

Chapter Four: Who are the key players in online abuse, and what can they do differently?

Imani Gandy, '#TwitterFail: Twitter's Refusal to Handle Online Stalked, Abusers, and Haters', Rewire News Group, 12 August 2014, https://rewirenewsgroup.com/article/2014/08/12/twitterfail-twitters-refusal-handle-online-stalkers-abusers-haters/.

Erin Woo, 'A Tech Whistleblower Helps Others Speak Out', *New York Times*, 24 November 2021, https://www.nytimes.com/2021/11/24/technology/pinterest-whistle-blower-ifeoma-ozoma.html.

Marianna Spring, 'I get abuse and threats online – why can't it be stopped?', BBC News, 18 October 2021, https://www.bbc.com/news/uk-58924168.

Ellen Judson, 'Gendered disinformation: 6 reasons why liberal democracies need to respond to this threat', Demos, https://demos.co.uk/blog/gendered-disinformation/.

Amnesty International, 'Women abused on Twitter every 30 seconds – new study', 18 December 2018, https://www.amnesty.org.uk/press-releases/women-abused-twitter-every-30-seconds-new-study.

Chapter Five: Building your digital self-care toolkit

'Beyoncé's Evolution', *Harper's Bazaar*, 10 August 2021, https://www.harpersbazaar.com/culture/features/a37039502/beyonce-evolution-interview-2021/.

Carla Nyst and Nick Monaco, *State-Sponsored Trolling: How Governments Are Deploying Disinformation as Part of Broader Digital Harassment Campaigns*, Institute for the Future, 2018, https://www.iftf.org/fileadmin/user_upload/images/DigIntel/IFTF_State_sponsored_trolling_report.pdf.

Chapter Six: Stepping up your digital security and self-defence

Glitch, 'Documenting Online Abuse', https://glitchcharity.co.uk/wp-content/uploads/2021/09/Glitch_Documenting_Online_Abuse_September2021.pdf.

Chapter Seven: Collective digital self-care and allyship

BT Sport, 'It's Time to Draw the Line', @foodandpsych, Instagram, 13 February 2021, https://www.instagram.com/p/CLPo6F_HEsB.

Rachelle Hampton, 'The Black Feminists Who Saw the Alt-Right Threat Coming', *Slate*, 23 April 2019, https://slate.com/technology/2019/04/black-feminists-alt-right-twitter-gamergate.html.

Maeve Duggan, 'Online Harassment 2017', Pew Research Center, 11 July 2017, https://www.pewresearch.org/internet/2017/07/11/online-harassment-2017/.

Department for Digital, Culture, Media and Sport, 'New laws to make social media safer', Gov.uk, 20 May 2018, https://www.gov.uk/government/news/new-laws-to-make-social-media-safer.

Statista, 'Number of monthly active Facebook users worldwide as of 4th quarter 2021', 14 February 2022, https://www.statista.com/statistics/264810/number-of-monthly-active-facebook-users-worldwide/.

Department for Business, Energy and Industrial Strategy, 'Workplace support for victims of domestic abuse: review report', Gov.uk, 14 January 2021, https://www.gov.uk/government/publications/workplace-support-for-victims-of-domestic-abuse/workplace-support-for-victims-of-domestic-abuse-review-report-accessible-webpage.

Paul Graham, How to Disagree, https://www.paulgraham.com/disagree.html.

Elaine McCallig, 'John Lewis responds after Black family in Christmas advert hit with racist abuse', indy100, 5 November 2021, https://www.indy100.com/viral/john-lewis-christmas-advert-racist-abuse-b1952220.

Clea Skopeliti, 'UK supermarkets unite after Sainsbury's advert prompts racist backlash', *Guardian*, 28 November 2020, https://www.theguardian.com/world/2020/nov/28/uk-supermarkets-unite-after-sainsburys-advert-prompts-racist-backlash.

Chapter Eight: Mistakes and reflections – what my journey so far has taught me

I Weigh with Jameela Jamil [podcast], December 2020, https://podcasts.apple.com/gb/podcast/seyi-akiwowo/id1498855031?i=1000501290961.

She can. She did. [podcast], Season 5, Episode 1, 30 March 2021, https://shows.acast.com/shecanshedid/episodes/episode-1-with-seyi-akiwowo-founder-of-glitch.

Glitch, 'The death of Sir David Amess MP and online anonymity', Medium, 20 October 2021, https://medium.com/@glitchuk_/the-death-of-sir-david-amess-mp-and-online-anonymity-ca3906e674cd.

Business Standard, '36% of call centre agents have been threatened with violence: Study', 10 September 2021, https://www.business-standard.com/article/companies/36-of-call-centre-agents-have-been-threatened-with-violence-study-121091000102_1.html.

Mirage News, 'Fixing Glitch: time to take a public health approach to tackling Online Abuse', 21 April 2021, https://www.miragenews.com/fixing-glitch-time-to-take-a-public-health-546675/.

Resources

Allyship and community

Mia Birdsong, *How We Show Up: Reclaiming Family, Friendship, and Community*, Hachette Go, 2020.

The Black Curriculum, https://theblackcurriculum.com/downloads.

Shon Faye, *The Transgender Issue: An Argument for Justice*, Allen Lane, 2021.

Glitch, 'A Little Means a Lot', https://glitchcharity.co.uk/wp-content/uploads/2021/09/Glitch_Online_Active_Bystander_ALMAL_Sept2021.pdf.

Nova Reid, *The Good Ally: A Guided Anti-Racism Journey from Bystander to Changemaker*, HarperCollins, 2021.

Layla Saad, *Me and White Supremacy*, Quercus, 2020.

Understanding online abuse and tactics

HeartMob, 'Social Media Safety Guides', https://iheartmob.org/resources/safety_guides.

Viktorya Vilk, 'Why You Should Dox Yourself (Sort Of)', *Slate*, 28 February 2020, https://slate.com/technology/2020/02/how-and-why-dox-yourself.html.

Women's Media Center, 'Shesource', https://womensmediacenter.com/shesource.

Mental health and self-soothing

Blurt, 'What Self-Soothing Means and 9 Ways to Do It', https://www.blurtitout.org/2019/01/03/self-soothing-means-9-ways.

Tara Brach, 'Resources: Working with Fear and Trauma', https://www.tarabrach.com/fear/.

Amelia Nagoski and Emily Nagoski, *Burnout: The Secret to Unlocking the Stress Cycle*, Ballantine Books, 2019.

Take Back the Tech, 'Self-Care: Coping and Healing', https://takeback-thetech.net/be-safe/self-care-coping-and-healing.

Documenting and reporting abuse

Department for Business, Energy and Industrial Strategy, 'Workplace support for victims of domestic abuse: review report', Gov.uk, 14 January 2021, https://www.gov.uk/government/publications/workplace-support-for-victims-of-domestic-abuse.

Department of Health / SafeLives, 'Responding to colleagues experiencing domestic abuse: Practical guidance for employees experiencing domestic abuse', https://safelives.org.uk/node/573.

Glitch, 'Documenting Online Abuse', https://glitchcharity.co.uk/wp-content/uploads/2021/09/Glitch_Documenting_Online_Abuse_September2021.pdf.

Glitch, 'Resources', https://glitchcharity.co.uk/resources.

National Democratic Institute, *Addressing Online Misogyny and Gendered Disinformation: A How-To Guide*, National Democratic Institute for International Affairs, 2021, https://www.ndi.org/sites/default/files/Addressing%20Gender%20%26%20Disinformation%202%20%281%29.pdf.

Online SOS, 'Threat Modeling', https://onlinesos.org/resources/action-center/threat-modeling.

Police UK, 'How to Report Stalking or Haraassment', https://www.
police.uk/advice/advice-and-information/sh/stalking-harassment/
how-to-report-stalking-harassment.
Stop Online Abuse, 'Resources', https://www.stoponlineabuse.org.uk.

Helplines and support services in the UK

Cybersmile Foundation, https://www.cybersmile.org/what-we-do/
online-abuse-support – anti-cyberbullying and digital well-being charity.
Galop, https://galop.org.uk – LGBT+ anti-abuse charity.
Muslim Women's Network, https://www.mwnuk.co.uk/Helpline_181_
c.php – national specialist faith and culturally sensitive helpline.
National Stalking Helpline, https://www.suzylamplugh.org/pages/
category/national-stalking-helpline – for victims of stalking.
Refuge, https://www.nationaldahelpline.org.uk – 24-hour national
domestic abuse helpline.
Revenge Porn Helpline, https://revengepornhelpline.org.uk – for adult
victims experiencing intimate image abuse.
Rights of Women, https://rightsofwomen.org.uk – organization helping women through the law.
Stop Hate UK, https://www.stophateuk.org – 24-hour anti-hate-crime
reporting service (includes a text relay and BSL service).
TellMAMA, https://tellmamauk.org – for reporting anti-Muslim incidents and attacks.
Victims Choice, https://victimschoice.org.uk – helps find victim services in your area.
Women's Aid, https://www.womensaid.org.uk/information-support –
national charity working to end domestic violence and abuse against
women and children.

Other dope organizations and projects

Antisemitism Policy Trust (UK), https://antisemitism.org.uk.

Association for Progressive Communications (Global), https://www.apc.org.

AWO Agency (Europe), https://www.awo.agency/about/.

The Black Curriculum (UK), https://theblackcurriculum.com.

Braving the Backlash: How Brands Can Stand Up to Hate Speech Online (UK), https://wearesocial.com/uk/blog/2018/08/braving-the-backlash-how-brands-can-stand-up-to-hate-speech-online/.

Chayn HQ (Global; particularly Pakistan and India), https://www.chayn.co.

The Diana Award (UK), https://diana-award.org.uk.

Digital Freedom Fund (Europe), https://digitalfreedomfund.org.

Digital Sisters/Sistas Inc. (US), http://digitalsistas.org.

Elect Her (UK), https://www.elect-her.org.uk.

End Violence Against Women Coalition (UK), https://www.endviolenceagainstwomen.org.uk.

European Women's Lobby, *#HerNetHerRights*, https://www.women-lobby.org/IMG/pdf/hernetherrights_resource_pack_2017_web_version.pdf.

The Everyday Sexism Project (UK), https://everydaysexism.com

Feminist Internet (UK), https://www.feministinternet.com.

Hope Not Hate (UK), https://hopenothate.org.uk.

National Democratic Institute (UK), https://www.ndi.org/regions/stub.

PEN America (US), https://pen.org.

Pollicy (Africa), https://pollicy.org.

Right To Be (previously known as Hollaback!), www.righttobe.org.

#ShePersisted (Global), https://www.she-persisted.org.

Take Back the Tech (Global), https://takebackthetech.net.

Tall Poppy (US), https://www.tallpoppy.com.

TrollBusters (US), http://www.troll-busters.com.

Social media safety, support and security pages

Facebook: https://www.facebook.com/safety.

Instagram: https://help.instagram.com.

Pinterest: https://help.pinterest.com/en-gb/article/we-protected-your-account.

Signal: https://support.signal.org/hc.

TikTok, https://www.tiktok.com/safety.

Twitch: https://safety.twitch.tv.

Twitter: https://help.twitter.com/en/safety-and-security.

WhatsApp: https://www.whatsapp.com/safety.

YouTube: https://www.youtube.com/howyoutubeworks/policies/community-guidelines.